HUGH JOHNSON'S

HOW TO ENJOY

W I N E

❧

A FIRESIDE BOOK
PUBLISHED BY SIMON & SCHUSTER INC.

NEW YORK   LONDON   TORONTO
SYDNEY   TOKYO   SINGAPORE

FIRESIDE
Simon & Schuster Building
Rockefeller Center
1230 Avenue of the Americas
New York, New York 10020

Copyright © 1985 Mitchell Beazley Publishers
Text Copyright © 1985 Hugh Johnson
Illustrations Copyright © 1985 Mitchell Beazley Publishers

Edited and designed by Mitchell Beazley International Limited,
Artists House, 14–15 Manette Street, London W1V 5LB

Editor Christopher McIntosh
Designer Jill Raphaeline

Art Editor Roger Walton
Executive Editor Chris Foulkes

All rights reserved including
the right of reproduction
in whole or in part of any form

FIRESIDE and colophon are registered trademarks of
Simon & Schuster, Inc.

1 3 5 7 9 10 8 6 4 2

Library of Congress Catalog Card Number: 85-1748

ISBN: 0-671-72459-2 (Pbk.)

Typeset by Servis Filmsetting Ltd., Manchester
Printed and bound in Portugal
by Printer Portuguesa Lda

Hugh Johnson has also written and presented a video film,
'How to Enjoy Wine', on which this book is based.

CONTENTS

I
OPENING THE BOTTLE

A preliminary briefing on corks,
capsules and containers, together
with a description of the weapons used in
getting at the wine and the emergency
measures that must sometimes
be resorted to.

It has taken centuries – probably over 60 of them – to develop the perfect container for wine. Now we have it, the brilliant invention of the 17th century: the bottle and cork. A wine bottle is not just a container. It is a sealed vessel in which the wine, protected from the air, holds its complex potencies in readiness for the day when it is drunk. Once the bottle is opened the wine is exposed to the destructive effects of oxygen. There is no going back.

Pulling a cork therefore always has a touch of drama about it; sometimes more than a touch when the cork is unwilling to yield to muscle and corkscrew. To take an extreme case first, here is what you do if the cork proves totally immovable. Take the heaviest kitchen knife you can find. Hold the bottle in one hand, with the neck pointing away from you, and the knife in the other, with the blunt edge toward the bottle. Now run the blade up the neck as hard as you can, hitting the 'collar' of the bottle a terrific whack, and the neck should break off cleanly. It's a trick that can look impressive at a dinner party, but make sure you practise it first. For less recalcitrant corks the time-honoured corkscrew will do – although even this simple mechanism has countless variations.

CORKS: THE FIRST HURDLE

But first things first. Why are all fine wines plugged with what amounts to a lump of wood – or at least tree bark? It sounds unnecessarily primitive. The fact is that there is nothing to touch cork for the qualities that make an ideal wine plug. It is light, clean and almost impermeable. It is smooth, yet stays firmly in position in the neck of the bottle. It does not expand or contract with changes in temperature, it rarely rots and does not burn easily. Above all it is highly elastic. Squeeze it into the neck of a bottle using a corking machine and it will immediately expand to make an airtight and watertight fit.

What is this material that has proved such a boon to the wine trade – and sometimes such a strain to the muscles? Briefly, cork is the outer bark of the cork oak, *Quercus suber*, which grows most abundantly in Spain and Portugal. Before its bark is harvested, a cork tree must grow for 20 years; then the bark can be stripped about once in every decade. The sheets of bark are subjected to a long process of drying, treating with fungicide and storing before they are ready to be cut into those familiar plugs. A normal-sized cork is 24mm in diameter and will be squeezed into an 18mm neck. Champagne corks (31mm for a 17.5mm neck) are made from three layers of cork glued together, and a third of the cork bulges out over the top of the neck like the head of a mushroom. Cheaper corks are made from an agglomeration of dust and scraps.

Corks also vary in length. Basically, the longer a wine needs to be stored, the longer the cork. Many corks have information about the wine stamped on them – sometimes just the name of the region where the wine was made, sometimes almost as much detail as on the label.

Once in position, a good cork will last at least 25 years and sometimes as long as 50, although the best cellars

Virgin bottles exhibiting a variety of capsules. A capsule protects the rim and keeps the cork clean. Sheet lead is the best material, but plastic and aluminium foil are used for less expensive wines. The screw-cap is a combined seal and capsule.

will recork their old vintages at 25-year intervals. Only slowly will the cork become brittle and crumbly. It is essential, however, that the cork be kept wet by constant contact with the wine in the bottle. This is why wine bottles are always kept lying down.

Occasionally a small amount of fungus escapes the sterilization process and remains in the cork. When the infected part is in contact with the contents of the bottle the wine picks up the smell – a simple whiff of mould. Such a wine is said to be 'corky' or 'corked'. A rare problem, but when it happens there is no alternative but to jettison the bottle and open another one. Otherwise a good cork will normally present no problems. A poor cork, on the other hand, can be a menace. Italian wine bottles, for example, are notorious for having small, hard corks of low-grade material, jammed into necks that are narrower than normal, creating a difficult job when it comes to opening.

Any bottle of wine you buy will have the cork covered by a so-called capsule – partly for neatness or ornament, partly to protect the rim from chipping and the cork from getting dirty (or even eaten by mice). The best quality capsules are made of thin sheet lead, painted and usually embossed. It seems a pity to cut some of them, but it's the only way in. Some people like to take just the top of the capsule off, leaving the rest to decorate the bottle. I usually do this with the tall flasks that hold German or German-style wines – and often with any wine that I am going to put on the table in its own bottle. If I am going to decant, on the other hand, I always cut the capsule right off so that I can really see what I am doing.

Originally capsules were made by dipping the business end of the bottle in sealing wax. That's why some old corkscrews had a hammer-handle for chipping off the wax and a brush for getting rid of the messy debris. If you find yourself dealing with an old wax seal, take my advice and remove it over the kitchen sink or outside the back door – some place where chips of old wax won't matter.

Nowadays you see more and more plastic capsules on medium-priced wines. I hate them, not only for being plastic but also for being the devil to cut off. Some have perforated strips and tags, but these can easily break, so that you are left having to gouge off the capsule with a knife. Aluminium foil is another cheap capsule material used for bargain-basement wines. At least it has the advantage of being easy to take off.

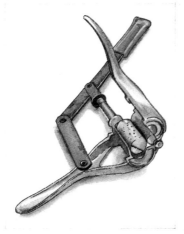

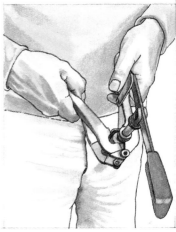

The invention of this gadget has reduced the business of corking to a simple four-stage operation. First load the machine with a well-soaked cork.

Then close the jaws like a nutcracker, compressing the cork to the diameter of the bottle neck.

Then of course there is the screw-cap. Traditionalists may shudder and swear that a cork is the only stopper for a fine wine, but the modern screw-cap is a perfect hygienic and airtight closure – and it has the tremendous advantage that you can easily put it back on again. For standard brands there is a lot to be said for screw-caps, and one day they will probably be used for fine wines as well.

No harm will come to any wine (except maybe very old wine) if you recork it and keep it in the refrigerator for a while. Almost all wines, red or white, and especially white wines, have a much longer refrigerator-life than most people realize. Three or four days carry very little risk. The simple way is to cut the top (the thinner end) off the original cork to get a clean end, and then drive it back in upside down with your fist. To keep the fizz in champagne there are some ingenious expanding bungs. Alternatively, there is a simple piece of jiggery-pokery you can do by inserting the handle of a small silver

Place the machine over the neck, one hand holding the machine, the other ready to operate the piston that will drive in the cork.

Finally push the piston down smartly, ramming the cork home. It will immediately expand to fill the neck, creating a perfect seal.

teaspoon into the bottle – why this keeps the bubbles in is something I have never fathomed.

CORKING MACHINE

The one-at-a-time corking machine, a simple lever that forces a cork into a bottle neck, is familiar to all home winemakers. I have used it until my hands were sore bottling a whole 60-gallon barrel of Cabernet from Chile a few years ago. Massive industrial production lines, with a rattling, jangling output of tens of thousands of bottles an hour, use the same simple principle: compress a cork into a cylinder the size of the bottle neck, ram it home and it instantly expands to a perfect, snug, liquid-and air-tight fit – and one that will last at least 25 years in good condition.

For hand-bottling purposes it makes the job much easier if you soften the corks well first by soaking them in clean water. The jaws of the corking machine open to admit the cork then squeeze it tight.

Asensible corkscrew pushes down on the bottle at the same time as it pulls up the cork. Human ingenuity has produced many corkscrew designs. Here are eight.

1 This ring-handled, folding corkscrew, like the classic T-shaped model, demands unnecessary exertion.

2 Victorian double-spiral. You insert it into the cork then twist the handle at the side to bring the cork out. The hammer-handle was for chipping away wax capsules, and the brush was for getting rid of the debris.

3 The butterfly. The levers rise as the screw is inserted. Then, as the levers are pushed down, the cork is drawn up.

4 Waiter's friend. The 'claw' grips the lip of the bottle, and the cork is levered out.

5 A more drastic solution. Compressed air is pumped through the needle so that the cork is forced out by pressure.

6 The zig-zag. It expands as the cork is drawn, exerting a powerful pull.

7 The butler's friend, so-called because the cork is not pierced and can therefore be re-inserted without detection. The prongs clasp the cork. To extract it you pull and twist.

8 In this design the metal cap fits over the neck of the bottle, and the screw is inserted through it. By continuing to twist you drive the cap against the neck, and the cork is forced out.

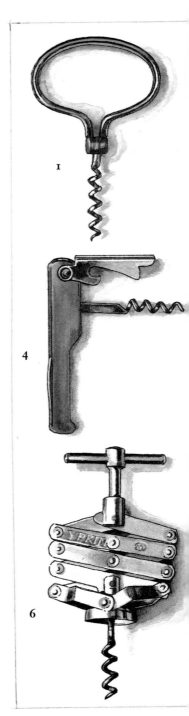

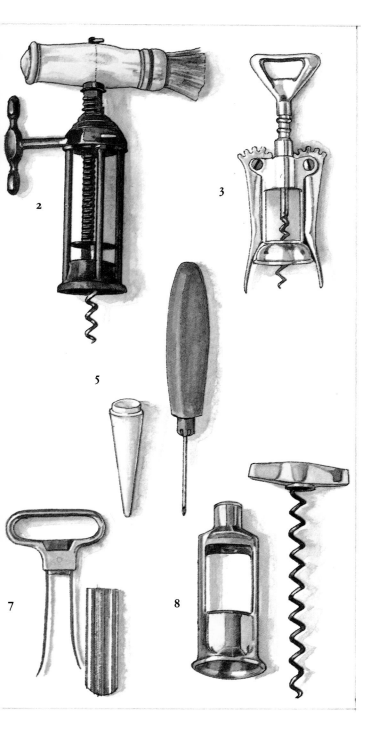

The first corks came into use as permanent bottle stoppers in the 17th century. Corking technology then consisted of a leather 'boot' to hold the bottle, and a 'flogger', a sort of wooden bat, to knock the cork in. Before their invention there was no satisfactory way of sealing bottles for long periods – which meant that wine could not be aged. One of the first cellar masters to take advantage of them was the 'father' of champagne, Dom Pérignon.

CORKSCREWS: CHOOSING AND USING

The essentially simple act of opening a wine bottle can be turned into an elaborate performance. Some waiters, for example, make a fetish out of holding the bottle in a gleaming white napkin – a wise precaution in the days when bottles sometimes broke during opening, but hardly necessary today. Unless you have a theatrical bent, it is better to avoid fuss and ritual.

Taking the cork out cleanly involves a little care. First cut off the capsule and, if necessary, give the top of the cork a wipe.

Insert the corkscrew in the dead centre of the cork without pushing hard. In this design a brass body guides the blade.

First remove the capsule, or cut it so that it is clear of the lip – this is especially important if the capsule is made of lead, which can affect the taste of the wine. Then if necessary give the lip and the top of the cork a quick wipe to remove any dirt or mould – here's where a cloth does come in handy. Now insert the corkscrew carefully, preferably not driving it right through the cork as this might cause fragments to fall into the wine – floating pieces of cork are harmless but unaesthetic. Draw the cork out with a slow, steady pull. A well-designed corkscrew, such as the Screwpull or the butterfly lever, will enable you to do this without great effort. Remember to keep the cork if you are planning to drink only part of the bottle and store the rest in the refrigerator. Finally, you may want to use your cloth again to give a last wipe around the inside of the rim. And there you are – ready to pour the first glass. With a sound cork and a good corkscrew it is as simple as that.

Turn the screw until the blade just reaches the bottom of the cork. This two-piece corkscrew then pulls the cork as you continue to screw.

A quick sniff will tell you if the cork is clean or, as in rare cases, contaminated by mould, giving the wine the same taste. Such wine is said to be 'corked' or 'corky'.

Corks that break off and stick in the neck are a familiar problem. One possible solution, shown here, is to insert the corkscrew at an angle, then push the cork against the neck while drawing it out.

The 'claw', a neat device for retrieving a broken cork that has fallen into the wine. It consists of three lengths of wire, hooked at the ends.

CORKS THAT BREAK OR WON'T BUDGE

These are another matter. Occasionally corks are too tight and break up (especially if the corkscrew is badly designed). Or they may have grown crumbly with age and need kid-glove treatment. Then again, they may be too loose and get pushed in. When this happens the wine usually splashes all over the person opening the bottle.

Supposing that, despite all precautions, a cork comes to pieces. One technique worth trying with a remnant out of reach in the neck is to put the screw in again at the most oblique angle you have room for, then push toward the side of the neck at the same time as pulling.

The idea is to push the claw down into the bottle, grabbing the broken cork, then tightening the grip by sliding a ring down the wires.

The remnant can then be fished out quite easily. The device will not work, however, if the cork has broken into many tiny fragments.

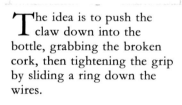

You squeeze the cork against the glass and hold it in one piece while gently pulling it out.

If that fails, and you are left with a cork in pieces in the neck and fragments floating in the wine, you might as well push the rest in. There is a fairly effective device made of three pieces of wire which will retrieve the bigger bits of cork easily enough from bottles with sloping shoulders. If it's a Bordeaux-type bottle with more pronounced shoulders, a quicker alternative is to push the cork right in and simply pour past it. You will get cork in your wine – at least in the first glass – but never mind; the wine won't taste any different.

The one wine you have to be really careful about opening is champagne. People who live in glass houses should watch out. There's a pressure of about 70 lb a square inch behind the cork, and if it gets loose it can be a really dangerous missile. The fancy dress on the top of a champagne bottle is partly a disguise for the very business-like wire cage that holds the cork in. The cork forms a mushroom shape because the top half isn't compressed into the bottle neck.

Chill champagne well before opening it, and try to avoid shaking the bottle more than necessary. If possible keep it horizontal until you are ready to open it. These precautions help to avoid an explosive opening and the loss of precious wine.

Have some glasses ready, find out where the wire is twisted, and hold the bottle angled away from you – not pointing at someone else or the windows. Untwist the wire and take it off with the top of the foil, keeping a wary thumb over the cork in case it flies.

Try twisting the cork. If it is too firm, ease it upwards with your thumbs while still being ready to stop it flying.

As soon as the cork budges at all, grip it firmly and twist the bottle with the other hand. Try to take the bottle away from the cork, and you should hear a nice little *phutt* of released gas. If there's a loud pop, then you are a beginner.

You want to get the fizz into the glasses quickly without it rising in a mass of froth or spilling over. The answer is to start each glass with an inch of wine. That quickly settles down, then go around again, filling them up.

Would anyone really use red-hot tongs to open a bottle of wine? They sound a desperate measure. In fact they are a well-tried way, when the long cork in an ancient bottle of vintage port has become too crumbly for a corkscrew. First the tongs are heated till they glow in an open fire or in a gas flame.

Next, they are clamped around the neck of the bottle, fitting just above the bottom of the cork, and held tight shut for at least half a minute to heat a ring of glass.

OPENING VINTAGE PORT
WITH FIRE AND FEATHER

Bottles of vintage port can present special problems in opening. They are designed to be stored for many years for the raw grape juice and brandy to 'marry' and mellow. There is still a convention (more honoured in the breach than the observance) of laying down a case of port when a son is born, to be drunk on his twenty-first birthday. The neck of a vintage port bottle is tall and slightly bulging, and is fitted with a very long cork. If the bottle is stored for longer than about 25 years the cork can become soft and crumbly, tending to break up when you pull on it with the corkscrew. In this condition a cork is virtually impossible to extract in the normal way. Sometimes the technique of inserting the

Now without a pause you stroke the bottle neck just where the tongs encircled it with a feather that has been dipped in cold water (a damp cloth will do). With the change of temperature the neck cracks right through in a clean ring.

Finally you take a firm grip of the top of the neck and lift it neatly off, bringing the cork with it, as easily as a stopper. The cork will have stopped any glass from falling into the wine – but usually the crack is so clean there are no chips.

corkscrew at an angle will work, but otherwise more extreme measures are required.

You can, of course, resort to the 'decapitation' procedure described at the beginning of this chapter. But a less violent and more elegant way is to use a pair of port tongs (of the kind shown here). You heat them in an open fire or gas flame until they are red-hot, clamp them around the neck of the bottle and leave them there for half a minute. Then wipe the same spot with a damp cloth or – for a touch of style – a feather dipped in water. A faint snapping sound will be heard, and you will know that the neck has split in a neat circle. Then you just lift off the top like a stopper, bringing, unless you are unlucky, the whole cork with it. An impressive trick – but the main thing is that it works.

II
STORING THE WINE

*A*ll you ever really needed
to know about keeping a
wine cellar — even in a wardrobe. Why,
when and for how long to store wine.
An unfamiliar use for a can of hair
spray. And how to remember where you
have put which bottle.

Do you mean I can't open it now? That depends. Any wine that's worth a premium is worth storing, at least for a few months and maybe for years, depending on the properties of the individual wine.

The thing to remember is that wine is alive – if you ever meet a dead wine you will know it without being told. Being alive, it reacts to certain physical stimuli (such as violent movements and extreme heat and cold). It also passes at a faster or slower rate through the process of ageing. The mark of the best wine is that it has the longest life span – given that it is kept in suitable conditions.

Everyday wine, the bulk stuff, is blended to be at the best age for drinking (usually very young) when it is bottled. Good examples of everyday wine are robust enough to live on happily for, say, six months to a year. In fact, really well-chosen everyday wines can show a distinct touch of class if they are given a chance, by being carefully stored for a year or so.

Don't assume, though, that old jug is better than new jug. The opposite is more likely to be true. But if a jug red strikes you as being unusually tasty for the category where most reds are fairly thin, give a few bottles a chance to prove themselves. Instead of opening them in quick succession drink them at intervals of, say, a month or six weeks. You will soon be aware whether you are watching improvement or decline – and drink the rest or keep it accordingly.

I would hesitate to keep low-price whites on the same principle. Freshness (if they have it) is often their main virtue. So don't throw it away. Drink them up while they are still at their best.

At the premium level things are, or should be, different. Whenever you pay more for a distinct style, whether it is an Appellation Contrôlée or something from a highly regarded winery, you are paying for extra flavour, extra strength and vitality, extra nuance. In living wine these qualities are rarely predictable. For several months after bottling, fine wines are often in a sort of state of dumb shock. They seem to sulk. Open them then and you will be disappointed by the lack of fragrance and flavour.

It is worth, therefore, keeping all newly made and bottled fine wines for at least three or four months before even thinking of sampling them. Remember, wine is alive. Shipping it a distance to your home can give it the sulks almost as much as the original bottling can. Mature wines don't need such a long recovery period as new ones, but try to give them a few weeks at least.

Beaujolais Nouveau is generally held to be the great exception: at its best for breakfast the day after bottling (and maybe a helicopter ride into the bargain). Don't believe the myth. There is no doubt that good Beaujolais Nouveau improves steadily through Christmas and the whole of its first winter. Just see how silky it is at Easter and you will realise what you would have missed by drinking it all in the autumn.

The rewards for storing the grander grades of wine

increase in direct proportion to their initial quality. First-growths are traded, as well as drunk, because they are known to have the potential to live, gradually improving, developing and finally (when rarity adds to their value) declining over a period that can last anything between ten and 100 years.

KEEPING A CELLAR

If nothing can quite equal the atmosphere of an ancient underground cellar, all beams and cobwebs, the word and the fact today are usually interpreted in terms of some cramped space above ground, often of a makeshift nature.

What is important, and what still makes a hole in the ground the best of all places to store wine, is its natural conditions of cool, even temperature, dark, calm and a certain degree of humidity. With ingenuity these conditions can be achieved in a cupboard under the stairs, in the back of a garage . . . anywhere that can be insulated. Most modern wine cellars are contrived in less than ideal conditions. But don't be put off. Given reasonable consideration most wines survive.

The first requirement is that the wines be kept at a reasonably even temperature, neither too warm nor too cold, but somewhat below normal room temperature. This means anything between 7° and 18°C (45° and 64°F). The ideal is about 10°C (50°F). At 10°C your white wines will be kept constantly at the right temperature for serving, and the red ones will mature slowly but steadily. Slow and moderate fluctuations in temperature will not harm the wines, but sudden and violent ones will age them prematurely.

A thermometer is a useful piece of equipment for any wine cellar, since the right temperature is essential for creating good storage conditions. If few people can afford a custom-built, temperature-controlled cellar, most of us can find ways of keeping our wine at an acceptable degree of coolness, even if it means using a cupboard next to an outside wall. The scale shows Fahrenheit on the left and Centigrade on the right.

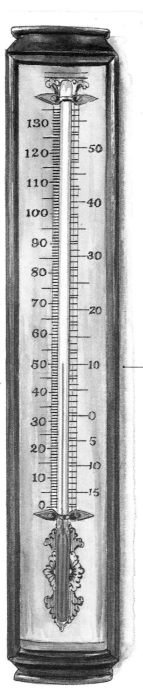

Average room temperature – all right for human beings, but a little too high for wines.

Domestic refrigerator temperature – somewhat too cold for long-term storage.

Ideal cellar temperature. At this degree white wines will stay cool enough for serving, while reds will mature slowly but steadily.

In a humid cellar labels are liable to moulder away, like the one on the left. When this happens the identity of the wine is lost, and its commercial value disappears. One ready solution is a can of hair-spray or artist's fixative. A quick squirt over the label creates a permanent seal.

The classic underground wine cellar is not only cool but also dark and rather damp. Darkness is important because light will age a wine prematurely, especially if it is in a clear glass bottle – and ultraviolet rays will penetrate even a dark-tinted bottle. This is why, incidentally, you should never buy a fine wine off a brightly lit shelf in a store.

Moderate humidity keeps a cork in a good, pliable, resilient condition and stops it shrinking. If your storage room is unduly dry you can install a humidifier or improvise one in the form of a bowl of moist sand.

Too much humidity will not damage the wine, but it soon rots cardboard boxes and encourages mould on labels. The label is the gauge of the value of a bottle; you can't afford to let it moulder. If this becomes a problem there is a very simple solution: before you store a bottle give the label a squirt with some scentless hair lacquer or artist's fixative. It makes a permanent seal against damp.

The cellar should not suffer from the shakes. Calm repose without vibration is ideal for wine. In practice this is unlikely to be a problem in most homes. The small

Most people have to improvise their wine cellar from any available space in the home. Here a fireplace with a blocked-up chimney makes a convenient place for storing wine – limited in space, but at least the bottles are easily accessible.

vibrations encountered in an average house do no harm.

Let us suppose that your dwelling, like most people's, is cellar-less (in the traditional sense). How do you set about creating the best storage conditions for your wine? Your first problem is likely to be space. If you live in your own house it is sometimes possible to have a small cellar dug out – say under the floor of your garage. Failing that, you will have to make do with any available space where conditions are approximately right. Ideally you should find a small room or cupboard with an outside wall and insulate it generously. A fireplace with a blocked-up chimney is a possible solution. Limited in space, though. So is the bottom of a wardrobe. Another solution is to have a temperature-controlled storage unit; a kind of refrigerator about 4°C (39°F) warmer than the normal. For wine drinkers who have small apartments these may be the best answer. A traditional wine merchant will usually store (for a small fee) wine you have bought that won't fit into the cabinet, until you have room for it. The step beyond (and may you reach it soon) is an insulated, air-conditioned room.

KEEPING TRACK OF YOUR STOCK

It's a fair bet that once you have put a bottle away you will forget which slot you put it in. If you are to use your precious storage space with any efficiency at all a bit of book-keeping is essential. It needn't be difficult. Just give each row of your wine rack a number or letter (say, numbers horizontally, letters vertically). Each aperture

T his wine rack is arranged according to a grid system – letters vertically, numbers horizontally. When a

will have, as it were, a map reference consisting of a letter and a number. Whenever you put a bottle away simply write this reference in your notebook. If you do this you can even scatter a dozen bottles of one wine all over the cellar, wherever there happens to be a vacant slot, and find them all again easily. Any other method wastes precious space.

bottle is stored away the grid reference is entered in the cellar book, making it a simple matter to retrieve the bottle.

A cellar record book is essential for keeping track of any stock of more than a few cases of wine. This is the first purpose-made and printed cellar book known, recording the stock in an English nobleman's London cellar between 1760 and 1780.

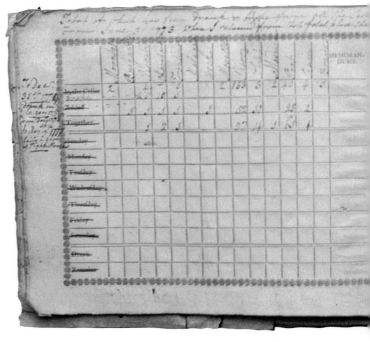

The butler made daily entries recording a remarkable consumption, particularly of sherry, port

HOW LONG MUST I KEEP IT?

Although it is certainly true that far more good wines are drunk too early in their lives than too late, it is a bitter moment when you open a bottle and find it 'over the hill', faded, dried-out or flattened by age. Like missing a plane. So how long should you keep it?

There never was, and never will be, a cut-and-dried answer. The better sort of vintage chart tells you, in

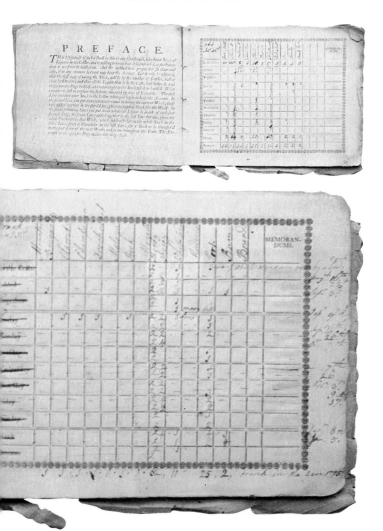

and Madeira. Any notebook can easily be tabulated to record what you buy, store and consume.

general terms, when each vintage of each important region is nearing maturity. My *Pocket Wine Book* (in the USA *The Pocket Encyclopedia of Wine*) goes into wine-by-wine detail annually for nearly 2,000 individual wines. But let us suppose you have had a bottle for three, or five, or ten years and you want to know whether there is any percentage in keeping it longer. Read the charts, read the wine magazines. But also look at the bottle.

Red wines reveal a lot about themselves by their colour, even through the glass of the bottle. Young wines are clearly red to purple, varying in intensity from vintage to vintage, region to region and grape variety to variety.

If a red wine is impenetrably dark when held against a light bulb, the odds are that the flavour will be impenetrably intense, young and harsh. Look at a few bottles against the light and you will quickly learn that young Bordeaux, for example, is usually darker than young burgundy. Look at ten-year-old bottles of both and you will see how both have faded away from purple

You can tell a lot about the contents of a bottle by holding the neck between yourself and a 60-watt lamp. The relative hue, in the range of purple-red-brown-orange, becomes obvious. This bottle of burgundy is typically pale, with its colour advancing from red towards orange.

and toward red-brown. Prime time is usually when the wine is just moving across the spectrum of red into faint hints of brown or orange.

White wines move the other way – from very pale to straw to gold to amber. Only such noble sweet wines as Sauternes should ever be kept beyond the transition from straw to gold – which is easy to see through the (usually clear glass) Sauternes bottle. Respect a fine white wine's pedigree, and give it at least a year, preferably two or three – but then drink it. Believe what you read about serious red wines. It is a crying shame to drink them while they are still pubescent.

In contrast to the burgundy on the left, this Bordeaux of the same age (ten years) has lost its original dense purple hue but remains a full red with only a hint of browning. It is in about the middle of its lifespan, certainly drinkable now but with plenty of years left to improve further.

A wine cellar with traditional 'bins', large apertures designed for holding many bottles of the same wine in the days when it was common to buy in bulk.

STACKS AND RACKS

Old-fashioned cellars were designed with so-called 'bins' – simple shelves on which you piled the bottles as many as ten deep, because you bought your wine by the barrel and it was all the same. Even the label is a relatively new invention. A case of port delivered to my cellar in 1965 had no labels. Each bottle just had a white paint mark to show which way up the bottle should be. You can use a label in the same way: keep the label uppermost and any sediment will be at the bottom when you come to pouring. You will also be able to read the label easily.

The trouble with using the bin method today is that we don't buy vast quantities of one wine – indeed, few of us buy vast quantities at all. We may perhaps have only one bottle of a particular wine, and we need to be able to winkle out individual bottles easily. So we need racks.

A rack is simply a structure with a series of pigeon-

Smaller pigeon-holes are more practical for today's buyer, who needs to be able to retrieve individual bottles easily. The ones is this rack hold nine bottles each.

holes, each hole capable of holding one or more bottles. Racks with one-bottle apertures are the most useful all-rounders. Some are deep enough so that two bottles can be placed end to end in each aperture. I find it useful to have both this kind and the kind that holds 12 bottles for when I am buying a whole case of wine.

The commonest and best type of manufactured wine rack is made of wooden bars connected by galvanized metal strips in a modular system. Another system on the market is a spiral staircase made up of modular units in precast concrete, each unit containing bottle space. There are, however, any number of ways in which you can make your own bottle rack or improvise one. Short lengths of drainpipe are a practical and easy dodge. Even one of the ordinary carboard boxes in which you buy your wine from the merchant will make quite a serviceable temporary rack, provided of course that the room is dry.

SPACE-AGE CELLAR

The closest thing to a perfect cellar must be the Aladdin's cave of a celebrated collector of rare wine, Mr Tawfiq Khoury, in southern California. It is airy, cool, humidity-controlled, immaculately ordered – and huge. There is room for 40,000 bottles of all sizes, including special racks for every size from half-bottles to the largest, Impériales and Nebuchadnezzars. The wines range in age over about 100 years – with few, except perhaps champagne, intended for immediate drinking. It is a cellar for browsing, daydreaming, gloating if you like: an ideally designed repository for the finest wines, where their qualities are carefully recorded, with the opinions of all who taste them.

What are we to learn from this extravagant model? First, to plan ahead: to make calculations about what wines we will want (and can afford) to drink in their

This astounding cellar (*left*) in southern California has capacity for over 40,000 bottles, arranged for instant access. Air-conditioning provides conditions at least as good for maturing wine as any traditional cellar.

The cellar allows for storage of every shape and size of bottle up to the eight-bottle Impériale (*right*).

Each bottle is carefully catalogued and its position recorded (*left*). Attention to detail extends to the fact that all the racks are canted slightly backwards so that the neck of the bottle is higher than the base. Thus the sediment is encouraged to settle low in the bottle, making decanting easier.

maturity. The Khoury cellar holds far more fine wine than the Khourys will ever drink. Much of it is therefore an investment for resale when it reaches maturity. Its impeccable provenance will guarantee that it fetches the best prices.

The second lesson is one of orderliness and book-keeping. Not to be able to find a wine is bad. Not to be able to remember what it was like after you have tasted it is equally irritating. Cellar records should lead you straight to the bottle you are looking for, and remind you of when you last tasted it, and what you and your friends thought of it. They can also record where you bought it (and why), its price, what food you have eaten with it, what reference books and magazines have said about it, who you have drunk with, and when you consider it should reach its full maturity or start to decline and need drinking.

III

DECANTING

&

SERVING

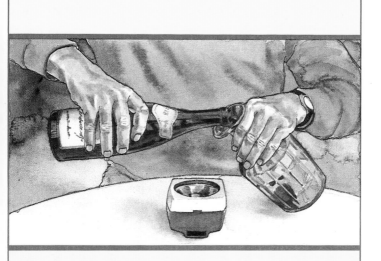

*T*he art of decanting (without the cant).
Should wine breathe or not breathe?
How to use an ice bucket — or a wet
newspaper instead. And a word about
glasses, good and bad.

43

The first English dictionary defined a 'decanter' as 'a glass vessel for pouring off a liquid clear from its lees'. Wine, in those days, was expected to be a bit murky at the bottom, whether in barrel or bottle. You decanted it into an elegant vessel for the table so your guests could admire its colour and clarity. Then you hung a label of silver or enamel around its neck to proclaim its contents. It all added up to dressing your wine to look its best at dinner – a procedure made less necessary today by clean-limbed bottles and eloquent paper labels.

Why, then, do we still decant? More to the point, why is it the modern custom to decant the best wines; those with the proudest labels? Mumbo jumbo and a surprising amount of acrimony surround what seems a very straightforward operation. It is the quickest way of starting an argument among wine buffs. Should you or shouldn't you decant wine X? If so, when?

Dr Johnson's original definition still points the way. If a bottle of wine has 'lees' or sediment (which nowadays only comes with age) it needs decanting. If you pour it from the original bottle, each backward and forward tilt as you go from glass to glass stirs up the muck and mixes it with the clear wine. In a bad case, especially with old red burgundy (burgundy can have very fine lees) as much as half the bottle will be thick and unpalatable unless you pour it carefully, in one uninterrupted movement, into a decanter.

The arguments start over what other effects decanting has on the wine. Pouring it from its bottle into a broader vessel, where it lies with a wide surface open to the air (whether or not there is a stopper), radically increases its access to oxygen. In a bottle it has been oxygen-starved. Now suddenly all its components can breathe in all the oxygen they have been missing. It would be surprising if there were not a fairly rapid change of scent and flavour.

Yet there is not, in most instances. Many authorities find themselves unable to tell any difference at all. Others (and this is the conventional French view) notice a slight decline in the vigour and personality of the wine. If a Frenchman decants wine at all it is usually just before drinking it. In a sense, you might say, he regards his glass as the decanter.

An equally well-established, specifically British, custom is purposely to expose wine to the air by decanting it several hours before drinking. The effect depends on the age and quality of the wine. Young reds being drunk before time has had its mellowing effect, still aggressive with tannin and acidity, tend to lose their bite and drink more smoothly. Mature ones give off more fragrance after a while in the decanter than when the bottle was opened. Low-quality wines have little to gain, but many become slightly more appealing. High-quality wines tend to develop their 'bouquet' slowly – but then they have much more to lose if they are opened too long before drinking. The key question, with no ready answer, is: at what point does the expensive fragrance, which is intended for your nostrils, begin to dissipate itself upon the ungrateful air?

The tools for the job: bottle, corkscrew, decanter and some light – a candle for atmosphere but a flashlight to really see what you're doing.

Into action. The essentials are a steady hand and a good viewpoint, with the light shining directly through the neck of the bottle into your eyes. Pour very gradually to start with.

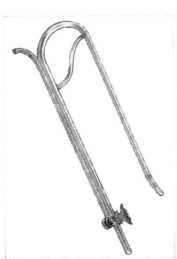

The idea of siphoning wine off its sediment, from bottle to decanter, came into fashion in the 1760s, with such beautiful pieces of silverware as this.

The siphon is thoroughly rinsed with water, then one end is put into the bottle. To start the wine running you suck briefly at the small priming pipe.

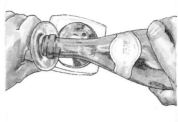

Nearly done. The essential is to make the pouring as far as possible one steady, uninterrupted movement. The object is to leave the sediment as undisturbed as possible until the last moment.

Time to stop. When a dark arrow-head formation begins to accelerate from the body of the bottle into the neck, stop pouring. Sediment not only muddies the wine; it can also impart a bitter taste.

As soon as you taste wine you stop sucking and turn on the silver tap to let the wine flow into a decanter, which you hold at a slightly lower level.

When the level in the bottle sinks to just above the sediment you turn off the spigot. Remember that the siphon is still full. Empty it over a glass.

What is certain is that no harm can come to vigorous young wine of good quality (a five-year-old Bordeaux of a good vintage, for example) by being decanted up to four or five hours before it is to be drunk – which is very convenient when you are making preparations for a dinner party. You can open the wine, taste it, decant it and think about its proper temperature well in advance of guests arriving. I wouldn't even hesitate to decant such a wine in the morning and leave it, stoppered, until the evening.

Real uncertainty starts with precious relics. It would be a shame to miss any of the perfumes that arise like incense from a classic wine in full maturity. This is the best argument for the French approach. If your friends are as intrigued as you are, you can go on finding different redolences for hours.

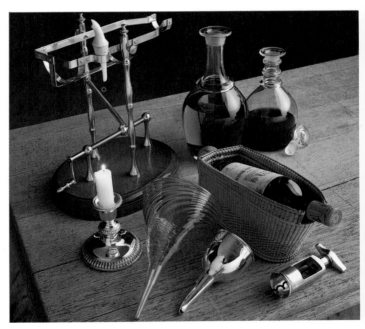

Wine has accumulated over the centuries some handsome paraphernalia for efficient and elegant serving. Shown here are some implements used in decanting. The Regency silver funnel has a spout turned sideways to make the wine run down the side of a decanter.

Decanting with the silver funnel, fitted with a piece of muslin as a filter.

Glass funnels can be used with muslin or coffee filter paper rinsed in water.

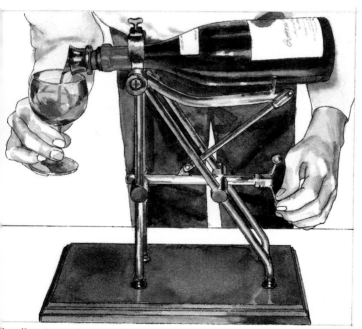

The decanting machine might be called the mechanical steady hand. A bottle is carried horizontally from its rack and opened on the machine. A very low-geared ratchet then tips it the precise amount to deliver a clear glass (or decanter) of wine.

49

Arange of decanters (left to right): an English Victorian silver-mounted claret jug; an English three-ring decanter of 1800; a mid 18th-century English decanter

a very unusual, probably Italian carafe with a 'marble' strip; a broad-bottomed 'ship's decanter'; a late 18th-century magnum decanter.

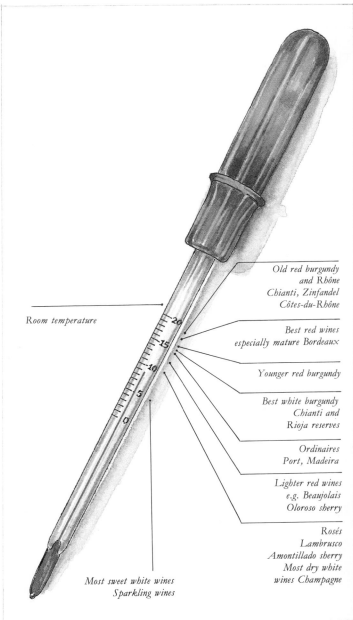

Room temperature

Old red burgundy
and Rhône
Chianti, Zinfandel
Côtes-du-Rhône

Best red wines
especially mature Bordeaux

Younger red burgundy

Best white burgundy
Chianti and
Rioja reserves

Ordinaires
Port, Madeira

Lighter red wines
e.g. Beaujolais
Oloroso sherry

Rosés
Lambrusco
Amontillado sherry
Most dry white
wines Champagne

Most sweet white wines
Sparkling wines

This gadget, the wineometer, is designed to be inserted into a bottle to test whether the wine is at the right temperature for drinking. The annotations show the ideal temperatures (in °C) for different types of wine.

GETTING THE TEMPERATURE RIGHT

If there is one single factor that makes or mars your full enjoyment of any wine it is its temperature in your glass. The ideal temperature depends on the weather as well as the wine. In summer all wines taste better a few degrees colder than they do in winter. The one cardinal rule is that any wine should be refreshing.

For most white wines, perfect storage temperature (the chill of a cellar) is ideal for drinking too. The kitchen refrigerator at around 44°F is a shade too cold for most white wines – except in summer when they will rapidly warm up anyway. In any case a refrigerator is a very inefficient way of chilling, simply because air is a bad conductor of heat. For the same reason a bucket full of ice on its own is also inefficient. The one really effective way of extracting the calories is total immersion in water and ice together, since water is the perfect conductor. Bear in mind that small ice cubes will melt quickly. The bigger the block of ice you use, the longer it will last. An ice bucket should be deep enough to immerse the whole bottle. If it isn't, put the neck in first, then reverse the bottle after a few minutes. Eight minutes in icy water will cool a bottle from 65° to 55°. In a normal refrigerator those ten degrees would take an hour to get rid of.

An unaesthetic but practical way of cooling wine when you are travelling without the benefits of refrigerators and ice buckets. Wrap the bottle in a wet newspaper or cloth and hold it by the open car window.

Once the bottle is cold there are some very pretty containers to keep it cool on the table. I have an Italian earthenware one that works like an old milk cooler. You soak it in water first, and evaporation keeps it cool. There is also a transparent, insulated model that works on the principle that cold air (off the bottle) lies on the bottom – more pretty than practical, I think. I prefer the freezer-bag version, which clasps the bottle in a jacket filled with a deep-frozen jelly.

What do you do if you are caught far from home, without any of these gadgets, dying of thirst and clutching a warm bottle of wine? In many a hotel bathroom I have wrapped the bottle in a wet towel and stood it in a draught. A rudimentary back-of-the-car technique on your way to a picnic is to roll the bottle in a well-soaked newspaper and hold it by an open window.

The perfect ice bucket is deep enough to drown a tall bottle. Fill the bucket with water and ice together, since water is the perfect conductor of heat.

Immersion in a bucket of warm water is the quickest way of warming red wine, but ideally you should let it reach the optimum temperature over as long a period as possible.

Unexpectedly, red wine is often harder to bring to the right temperature than white. 'Room temperature' or 'chambré' is the traditional gauge for red wine. But the phrase was coined before the days of central heating. It meant closer to 60° than the modern idea of comfort, which is 70° or more. At 70° or over reds lose their attractive 'cut'. They are no longer refreshing.

Your kitchen is the ideal place to let red wine gradually, over 12 hours or so, reach the perfect temperature. But what if you are in a hurry? Roasting the bottle in front of a fire is a hit-and-miss procedure. I prefer to use the controllable and direct method of a bucket of warm water. Water at 70° will raise the temperature from 55° to 65° in eight minutes, just as surely as icy water will lower it. If you are decanting the wine, decant it before you warm it.

Here is a selection of devices for lowering the temperature of wine. A Chinese fish bowl is as good a container as any (and better than most) for mass-cooling bottles. Use lumps of ice as big as you can make them in your deep freeze, and top up with water. Also in this picture is an earthenware milk-type cooler, using evaporation to lower the temperature, and a transparent, vacuum-filled container which keeps a ready-chilled bottle cool – admittedly not for very long.

Perfect drinking vessels. Each of these glasses – clear, simple and elegant – performs its function superbly. Note how in most cases the bowl is narrower at the top to hold in the bouquet. Familiar designs

GLASSES

You would think that a drinking glass, like a corkscrew, would be a simple thing to design. But I never cease to be amazed at the variety of impractical and downright hideous objects that pass for wineglasses. Take the champagne glass known as a 'coupe'. This is often used by caterers. It is quicker to fill. They libel Queen Marie Antoinette by saying that the original was modelled on her breast – the left one, I believe. Whatever the mould may have been, the glass is a horror. You can't avoid spilling from it, the champagne is flat and all its lovely smell is lost. You want to see the beautiful play of bubbles in champagne. And you want to have a decent ration that won't spill and leaves room for your nose to have its part of the fun.

Other types that are best avoided include the tinted kind that distorts the natural colour of the wine, the pretentious cut-glass thimble, the 'dock' and 'schooner'

include: (extreme left) the 'tulip' glass, ideal for champagne as it helps to retain the bubbles; (fourth from the right) the 'flute', another good champagne glass; (extreme right) the classic 'Paris goblet'.

that are used for sherry in old-fashioned pubs, and the glass with a flaring lip that depends on surface tension to even hold a decent portion – the only way to drink from the horrible thing without spilling is to bend double and sip the top off the contents.

I'm not being fussy. I only ask for three things in a glass. First, the bowl should be clear, not coloured, so that I can see what I am drinking – although the traditional tinted stems of Alsace and the Rhine are fine with their respective local wines and in the right setting. Second, the glass must be big enough to hold a proper ration without filling it to the brim. Third, the top should funnel inwards and not flare out. The glass used by experts in Bordeaux is close to ideal. It holds 6 fl oz (17cl) when filled halfway. The shape is elegant, the balance in your hand is just right. And, above all, when you hang your nose over the rim you get the full blast of the expensive aromas you have paid for.

The top half of the glass plays the part of a fume chamber. If you see wine professionals, growers or merchants swirling the wine around in their glasses and then inhaling before they taste, they are not being precious. They are using the walls of the glass to give the wine the maximum exposure to the air – thus to volatize its aromatic elements or, in plain language, to shake the smell out.

Another classic shape is the so-called Paris goblet, a standard piece of equipment in restaurants all over the world and not far short of ideal for either burgundy or claret.

Different wine regions have their traditional glass shapes and sizes. A quarter of a litre is reckoned a fair measure of German wine (which admittedly has a shade less alcohol than French). Old German Rhine-wine glasses had thick brown trunks – rather like the

Regional accents. Some of the long-established fine-wine areas have traditional glasses of their own. They may not improve the flavour of the wine but they add a touch of dialect. The ones shown here are, from left to right: Anjou, Alsace, the Rhine and Trier on the Mosel.

Rhinelanders' beloved trees – so that the wine had a reflected amber cast (it made it look older, thus better). But nobody would bang the table with one of the little diamond-cut glasses which the genteel citizens of Trier on the Mosel prefer to show off their equivalently delicate white wines.

The double-spouted Spanish *poron* is another traditional glass, designed so that you can drink from it without it touching your lips. One spout sends a stream of wine directly into your mouth while the other lets in air. I strongly suspect that when the Spanish invented this drinking vessel the whole point was to avoid the smell (and as much of the taste as possible). The wine had been kept in goatskins.

One thing is certain: the vessel you drink out of *does* affect your appreciation of the wine. So don't use just any old glass. Take a bit of trouble to find the right one.

A chamber of horrors. The three pretentious coloured glasses are bound to hide the colour of the wine. The ungainly champagne 'coupe' on the right will not hold a decent ration without spilling, and it ruins the sparkle and aroma of the prettiest wine of all.

IV

JUDGING WINE

*W*hat it's all about. The *moment* of
truth, or disenchantment, when you
raise the glass. How to appreciate the
look, smell and taste of the wine.
In short, how to savour every glass
to the full.

Why is it a mother's trick to hold her child's nose when there is medicine to swallow? The nose is the aerial for the organs of taste in your tongue, palate and throat. Cut off the aerial and you don't get much of a picture. It makes bad medicine tolerable. But it's a terrible waste of good wine.

Yet in effect this is what most wine drinkers do without thinking. Watch them. They give their glass a cursory glance (to make sure there's something in it), then it goes straight to their lips. The configuration of our faces obliges it to pass beneath the nose. But how often do you see it pause there, for the nostrils to register their message? Not often. The art of getting the most from wine is not complicated. But it does have to be learned.

Lesson one is to give it a chance. Any wine that is worth a premium is worth more than a clink and a swallow. How else do you justify the premium?

The art of tasting has been expanded and expanded to

Colour is an important criterion in judging a wine and will help to give an indication of its age. Only certain wines have the qualities necessary for ageing well. The majority are red wines, but there are certain whites that gain by ageing. Here, for example, are three bottles of fine Sauternes from good vintages: (left to right) 1975, 1970 and 1943. The colours reveal their different stages of maturation: pale gold, darker gold and a glorious rich amber. The older two are ready to drink and will in their different ways be splendid wines. The 1975 will, as its colour indicates, improve for some time yet. Red also changes colour with age, as the two glasses in the picture show.

fill volumes. Professional tasters stake their names, and large sums, on subtle distinctions that give grounds for investing in a wine's development far into the future. We, however, are talking about enjoyment, not analysis. We start, then, with a list of wine's distinctive characteristics and pleasures: points not to be missed.

Proof of the effect of age on the colour of red wine. Unlike white wine, a red will lighten rather than darken with age. Here are two red Bordeaux. The one on the right is still a rich, dark, purply red. The other, 14 years older, has turned a lighter, brick-red colour. Time has done something more than merely soften the older wine: it has brought out flavours within flavours.

APPEARANCE

The first is its colour, limpidity, viscosity, brilliance; its physical presence in the glass. It is the appreciation of the eye. A potent little pool of amber brandy, a glistening cherry tumbler of a young Italian red, a sleek ellipsoid of glowing ruby from Bordeaux or the crystal turbulence of champagne all carry different messages of anticipation. Each is beautiful. Each means something. Each is worth a close inspection. Gradations of colour can tell a practised eye the approximate age of a wine – sometimes even its vintage and the variety of its grapes. Each wine has an appropriate colour that experience can teach us to recognize. Red Bordeaux, to take one example, is nearly always a deeper red than burgundy. If it looks pale and thin the odds are that it will taste that way.

Texture, or viscosity, can be equally revealing. Fine wines with concentrated flavours, like blood, are thicker than water. Where they wet the sides of the glass they tend to cling, falling back in trailing drops that the Germans call 'church-windows'; the British, 'legs'.

AROMA

When a professional, a winemaker or merchant, swirls the wine around in his glass before sniffing and sipping he is deliberately aerating the wine as forcefully as possible. Your nose can only detect volatile substances. Some wines are naturally highly aromatic, others less so. The less aromatic it is, the more a taster has to, almost literally, shake the smell out of it.

The aromas of young wines are essentially the smell of the grapes, transmitted and intensified by fermentation. The grapes that make the best wines tend to have the most distinctive and memorable smells (aromas is the accepted word) from the moment they become wine. If the new wine is kept in oak barrels for a time the scent of oak overlays and partially conceals the grape smell for a while. After the wine is bottled and as it ages the components become less distinct and complex new aromatic substances form.

TASTE

Nose and mouth are not separate organs of sensation. The blocked nose impedes the mouth from tasting. What the nose detects by sniffing, the mouth will confirm by sipping. But at this third stage of enjoyment, holding the wine momentarily in your mouth before swallowing, all the elements in the wine that are not volatile reveal themselves. Flavour, as opposed to aroma (the trade term 'nose' is quite precise), is built up of acids, sugars, tannins, traces of minerals that can suggest, for example, saltiness. You cannot smell tannin or sugar – even though the aroma may suggest, by association, that they are there. Only the tongue, the palate and the throat can get the full feel of the wine; can judge its 'body' – the sum of all the flavours in a wine plus the warmth and potency of its alcohol.

Notice particularly what flavour is left after you have swallowed – and for how long. Poor wines leave either a nasty taste or none at all. Fine wines linger in departing sweetness. And great wines perfume the breath for a full five minutes, maybe more, after each sip.

1 Step one in sizing up a wine is to take a look at it against a white background such as a sheet of paper. Tilt the glass away from you so that you can see the colour, clarity and depth of the wine at the rim. With practice you can tell its approximate age.

2 Swirling the wine. This is a way of aerating the wine so as to release the volatile substances that create the aroma. Shaking the smell out in this way is especially necessary when the wine is low in natural aroma.

3 Putting the nostrils to work. A young wine will smell predominantly of the grape from which it was made. Older wines form complex aromas. Much of the pleasure of wine is lost if you skip this stage.

4 Assessing the first sip.
Taste is a combination of
what the nostrils have already
detected, plus the effect of the
alcohol and the non-volatile
elements – acids, sugars,
tannins and traces of minerals.
Only at this stage can you
judge the full feel of the wine.

5 'Chewing' the wine to
assess its 'body' – the sum
of its flavours combined with
the warmth and kick of its
alcohol. When you finally
swallow it, notice what
flavour lingers on your palate
and in the throat.

6 Strictly for tasting sessions
and not for dinner parties.
Spitting out each mouthful is
a way of sampling wines
without feeling the effects of
the alcohol. Experts develop
an accurate aim.

V

THE STYLES OF WINE

*S*ilk purses and sows' ears — or what it
takes to make a wine taste the way it
does — followed by eleven basic 'personalities'
of wine with a profile of each. Where
they are made, how they look and taste.
How to drink them to the
best advantage.

Wine, like Cleopatra, is infinite in its variety. There are no two places, cellars or cellarers which ever make an identical wine a second time. Some makers blend year with year, grape with grape, vineyard with vineyard for consistency. But it is the nature of wine to express more or less clearly the conditions of its making and the state of the raw materials. Add human tastes, skills and fallibility and you have a multitude that no man can number. Even to try to categorize wine into any sort of pattern is a tall order.

It is often classified or graded for quality, but to index wine's variety of flavour is much harder. The traditional way was by reference to a few 'classical' regions in France, Germany, Spain and Portugal, that supposedly set the styles for everyone to follow. It would be more accurate to say that the regions provided materials for merchants to adapt to the tastes of their customers.

Burgundy was supposed to be rich and smooth. But as nature seldom obliged, merchants arranged it that way by judicious blending. Red Bordeaux was christened claret for its lightness, but was in practice dosed with darker and heavier, usually Spanish, wine to satisfy the cravings of its main, northern European, market. Even the finest wines used to be cosmetically contrived to achieve as much predictability as possible. The habit has been retained by makers of sherry, champagne and port – and not only by them but by the important part of the wine trade that deals in standard brands.

In the wide world of fine or 'premium' wines, however, the reverse has become true. Individuality is considered a prime virtue. Wine lovers become almost more fascinated by the differences between wines than by the wines themselves.

PRIME FACTORS

What makes one wine different from another? In order of importance the prime influences are: (1) the intentions and skill of the winemaker, (2) grape variety, (3) climate, (4) weather, (5) the character of the soil, (6) how old or young the wine is.

The winemaker is almost always working within a tradition or convention rather than trying to introduce a brand new brew to the world. Usually (certainly in Europe) he is also working within a pretty strict set of rules. So the most important factor is the success or failure of his efforts.

Factor two, the grape, seems to become more and more important. Most people know that red wine and rosé wine are made of red grapes and that white wine is usually made of white grapes (to make white wine out of red grapes is an expensive eccentricity practised only when the price is right – for example in Champagne). But beyond such basic facts nobody, until a few years ago, seemed to know or care which grapes were used. At any rate they didn't talk about it. All that changed with the recent rise of the new wines of California, Australia and the rest of the new wine world. Winemakers there chose, as the way of identifying their better and best wines, to name the grape variety.

When the New World stopped calling any of its good reds burgundy and started specifying which one was made of Pinot Noir, the burgundy grape, attention was suddenly focussed on the grape, the basic taste and smell of the raw material for the first time. 'Varietal character' became a catch-phrase.

The point rapidly sank in that the sows' ears that won't make silk purses include most of the world's standard bulk-producing grape varieties. Only a score or so of 'noble' grapes are capable of producing good 'varietal' wine.

Factor three, the climate, matters less than it did. It used to be crucial in deciding how ripe the grapes were at picking time, and how fast they fermented, once picked. Very ripe grapes, fermented very fast, made bad wine. But along came refrigeration and changed all that. Wine-makers discovered how to pick at the ideal moment and keep the juice cool. The result: fine fragrant wines from hot climates – a drastic narrowing of the gap between the old fine-wine belt, where vintage time is cool, and the former bulk-wine belt, where it is hot.

Factor four, the weather, used to be decisive. It can still be. Serious frost, hail or rain at the wrong moment can wipe out a harvest. But the daily vagaries of temperature and humidity have less drastic effects than

A colourful array of many different wines (*left*) forms a background to a tasting session in Stockholm at the Systembolaget, the government organization through which all wine is sold in Sweden.

A winetasting (*right*) on the roof of San Francisco's Mark Hopkins Hotel. California, with its wide range of climatic conditions, produces examples of all the wine styles described in this chapter.

they used to, as grape-growers master techniques of spraying and draining their vineyards, pruning and training their vines to get the best out of even the worst seasons.

As for soil, factor five, a Frenchman will tell you it matters most of all. (But then he is defending his birthright.) A Californian will tell you a vine can grow good grapes almost anywhere. (But then that is just where he is planting it.) Soil does matter, especially from the point of view of drainage. But its direct link with the quality of the wine is hard to prove, and with wine style even harder. So only the top growths emphasize it.

WHEN AGE IS AN ADVANTAGE

Overlaid on top of all other considerations is the sixth factor: age. Far from being an automatic plus, age rapidly becomes a threat to the great majority of wines. They should really be sold with a 'Drink before. . .' date like milk. One year is a good age for most white wines, and up to two years for the great ocean of simple reds.

The only wines that need to be stored away before opening are those with concentrated flavour which are harsh at first, but which experience has taught will develop smoothness and complex flavours with age.

The price, if no other clues are available, will usually

tell you which they are. It stands to reason that few, if any, short-lived 'drink by . . .' wines are likely to change hands for much money. The blue-chip wines are all those which have a storage life of at least five and maybe up to 50 years, with the certainty or high probability that somewhere along the line between awkward youth and feeble old age, they will be marvellously satisfying to drink, with dimensions of flavour that no unaged wine can ever achieve.

ELEVEN BASIC MODES

These, then, are 11 broadly defined styles of wine, the results of differing combinations of our six factors, with typical examples and suitable uses.

Dry white wines with a simple flavour and without very distinct aromas

The equivalent of background music – agreeable but not a concert performance demanding your full attention. Youth and freshness are essential: these wines get tired quickly. They are often used as aperitifs, but can rapidly become boring without the addition of another flavour. Blackcurrant juice (cassis) is a favourite. With soda or Perrier they make a 'spritzer'. As partners to food they have almost limitless uses, rarely rising to gastronomic heights but always helping the appetite along with fish, cold meats, sausages, terrines, strongly garlicky dishes or curries which would smother fine wines. Serve them colder than better or more delicate whites.

Most branded dry whites, jug or carafe wines fit into this category. They are often made in large quantities in a warm climate, using 'neutral', that is unaromatic, grape varieties. Others in this group are Entre-Deux-Mers and other white Bordeaux, Muscadet, plain Chablis, Gaillac, most Sylvaner from Alsace, Aligoté from Burgundy and Mâcon Blanc. Italy's Soave, Verdicchio, Frascati, Pinot Bianco, Trebbiano, Orvieto secco and Sicilian whites can (and should) outshine this category, but in practice seldom do. California's cheaper whites nearly all belong here, whether called 'Chablis', Chenin Blanc, Mountain

A café terrace in Frascati, Italy, with a parade of the local wine. At its best, Frascati is a fragrant wine with a strong personality. More often it is simply a pleasant, unassertive accompaniment to food.

White or whatever. So do Australia's 'cask' and many other simple whites and South Africa's so-called 'Grands Crus'. Most Spanish whites belong here. Portuguese vinho verde is a light and fizzy version.

It is a wide spectrum without dramatic extremes – essential as a foundation for more exotic wine-drinking.

*Lightweight aromatic whites with grapey flavours
and more or less fruity/flowery scents*

Germany provides the models for this category. German wines are low in alcohol and correspondingly 'transparent' in flavour. The object is the scented crispness of fresh fruit, usually balanced with a degree of sweetness.

At the bottom end of the quality scale (for example much German 'Tafelwein') they can be plain watery – but at the top they can be the most exquisite of all wines for solo sipping. Their true role is to be drunk on their

A refreshment break during the vintage in

Alsace. Once part of Germany, Alsace makes white

own. Use them for wine parties, as aperitifs, while reading or writing letters or watching television – any time when refreshment and fragrance are more important than flavour and alcohol. In summer they are perfect garden wines, thoroughly chilled. In winter I like an after-dinner glass just pleasantly cool.

Good-quality German estate wines, whether from the Rhine or the Mosel, are the model for this class, and the Riesling is the model grape. Qualitätswein, Kabinett and Spätlese are the official descriptions. Brands such as Green Label and Blue Nun are safe, if unexciting.

vines whose style is partly Germanic, partly French.

They are stronger and drier than most German wines.

Quenching the thirst with a glass of the local produce in an Alsace vinyard.

France's aromatic answers are Rieslings and Gewürztraminers from Alsace (which are weightier in body and alcohol and usually drier) and light but much drier Sauvignon Blancs from the Loire (Touraine) and the Dordogne. Austrian Grüner Veltliner in its first year is one of the most appetizing examples. The Italian Tirol and Friuli and adjacent Slovenia (Yugoslavia) have a shot at this style of wine, though rarely as successfully as Australia with its exceptionally tasty Rieslings. New Zealand uses Müller-Thurgau and Gewürztraminer grapes to go for the same effect. England is doing better every year, mainly with Müller-Thurgau. California's freshest Gewürztraminer and Riesling is sometimes in this style, but more often full-bodied; very much wines for tasty food.

Sparkling wines, with champagne as the boss
There is an enormous range of quality and style between a plain white wine with bubbles and the sinful opulence of the silkiest champagne. Scarcely a wine region in the world has not attempted recently to enter this huge growth area by producing its own sparkling wines. The best non-champagne sparkling wines come from Burgundy (Crémant de Bourgogne), the Loire (Crémant de la Loire), Alsace (Crémant d'Alsace), south-west France (Blanquette de Limoux), Catalonia (top Codorníu and Freixenet wines), northern Italy (Lombardy,

A roadside tasting of Mosel wine in Germany. The Germans excel in producing light, aromatic wines, low in alcohol and ideal for drinking on their own.

Trentino, Piedmont), Germany (high-grade Sekt), California – where several French champagne firms have established cellars – and Australia. They all use the champagne method (*méthode champenoise*) and proclaim it on their labels. Other sparkling wines can be fun, but are usually more so when flavoured with fresh orange juice or a drop of syrup (cassis, grenadine or strawberry). The ultimate 'fun' wines are sweet sparkling muscats, with Asti Spumante at their head.

Assertive, full-bodied dry whites with positive characters derived from the best grapes and/or maturity

White burgundy, the marriage of Chardonnay grapes and small oak barrels, is the epitome of this class. But all France's best dry whites have the same profile: nose-filling scents, mouth-filling flavour, moderate alcohol, appetizing succulence without distinct sweetness. Their aim and purpose is to accompany food. They are fatiguing to drink without it. Their flavour is as strong as that of most red wines; don't lose it by over-chilling.

The list is long, but starts with the Chardonnay grape almost everywhere it is grown. It needs at least a year in bottle, usually two or more, to reach its full flavour. High quality mature wines from the following grapes and areas can all be bracketed here as the best meal-time whites, with almost any savoury food: Chardonnay, Riesling, Sauvignon Blanc, Gewürztraminer, Pinot

G rapes harvested in Alsace stand ready to be taken by horsepower for pressing. When an Alsace wine bears the name of a grape, such as Sylvaner, Riesling or Gewürztraminer, it must be 100% of that variety.

Gris, Chenin Blanc, Sémillon, Marsanne, Viognier, Furmint (all these are grapes) from Burgundy, Alsace, Graves, the upper Loire (Sancerre and Pouilly), Anjou (Savennières), the northern Rhône, Catalonia, Italy, Austria, Hungary, Yugoslavia, Bulgaria, coastal California, Australia, South Africa. Also the best white Riojas and classic examples of Frascati, Soave, Cortese di Gavi, Pinot Grigio, Pomino, etc. Montilla and manzanilla finos from Andalucia can be included, and so can the old-fashioned characters of Austro-Hungary: Szürkebaràt, Rotgipfler, Ruländer.

Sweet white wines

These, like sweet dishes, come at the end of most people's meal-plan. Not all, though; the Bordeaux idea of heaven is not caviar to the sound of trumpets, but foie gras to the sip of Sauternes – the sweetest wine with the richest food.

Oddly, where most wines taste best with complementary or not dissimilar food, sweet wines show to their best advantage with contrasting food, or no food at all.

However good a Sauternes may be, it can't add much to a beautiful apple tart, all butter and caramelized fruit. But it illuminates a savoury foie gras and faces up to strong and salty cheeses as no red wine can do.

Sauternes (and its colleague Barsac) is the best of sweet table wines, leading a fairly limited field. The other runners are 'liquorous' (sticky and golden) wines from the neighbouring Bordeaux villages of Ste Croix du Mont, Loupiac and Cérons, Monbazillac from the Dordogne not far away, and certain Loire wines made in rare autumns in Anjou (Bonnezeaux, Quarts de Chaume) and Vouvray. Alsace makes some late-picked Rieslings and Gewürztraminers that can be used in the same way. So does Austria with its Ausbruch and Beerenauslese wines from the Burgenland, and likewise Hungary with its Tokay. All these are powerfully flavoured and fairly high in alcohol.

In contrast the fabulously rare, very sweet wines of Germany, Beerenausleses and Trockenbeerenausleses, are low in alcohol and, like their drier counterparts, are unquestionably best sipped after or between meals.

French vin ordinaire in a café setting in Burgundy and (*right*) Berry. In France such wines are always on tap

The most aromatic of all sweet wines are made of muscat grapes, in most degrees of sweetness and strength ranging from an almost treacly character (as in the five-star brown liqueur muscats of north-east Victoria, Australia) to wines that are so delicate that they have to be kept under refrigeration – a speciality of one or two Napa Valley growers.

The lower Rhône valley produces an admirable sweet-but-not-heavy version, Beaumes de Venise. Roussillon in France and Tarragona in Spain make stronger wines. Sicily, Portugal and Russia all make delicious brown muscats, but without ever really putting them on the map. The world used to use much more sweet wine than it does today. Isolated examples of excellent ones crop up in Cyprus (Commandaria), France (Banyuls), Tarragona (Priorato Dulce and Pajarete), Malaga, Marsala and in California's Angelica.

Rosé wines, from camisole pink to onion-skin orange
There is no prestige in being a middle-of-the-roader, but you collect a lot of friends. Pink wines are made as

82

– rather like the Englishman's cup of tea. To be refreshing they should be served on the cool side.

though they were going to be red until the winemaker read in his paper that red was out of style. He makes a white wine of red grapes, stained with their skins but not toughened with their tannins. If the grapes are aromatic, the rosé can be fabulously so. Burgundy's one rosé, Marsannay, can smell more ravishingly of new-born Pinot Noir than any wine. Cabernet Sauvignon makes excellent rosé in California and Cabernet Franc in Anjou. Grenache, a sweet but unscented grape, makes strong but unscented rosé. Tavel, the one famous example, always strikes me as making the best of a bad job.

Broadly, you can divide rosé into pink-with-a-hint-of-blue (var. camisole) and pink-with-more-than-a-hint-of-brown (var. onionskin). Anjou typifies the first, Tavel the second. Wines that are just off-white, the palest of pinks, as though by mistake, are called by the French 'vins gris' – grey wines. Champagne, made with Pinot Noir, used to be not infrequently faintly grey. But pink champagne today is stained a clear, bright pink by adding a dose of the region's red. It is one of the prettiest and most luxurious of all wines.

Fresh grapey young reds

Beaujolais is the first name in a class of wine that grows more and more fashionable. If the most 'serious' white wines invade red territory with their savoury richness, these most frivolous reds cross the (anyway vague) border into a class of flavour associated with white wine. Like whites they rely on acidity for their bite and liveliness (reds have acidity too, but back it up with tannin). In the conventional ordering of several wines, red comes after white. You can treat these wines as young whites – and serve them almost as cool. Above all don't try to age them: the bottom falls out. Without their simple childlike vitality they are dull and thin. Drink them young, with food (any food except highly savoury gamey dishes) or without. They go as well as white wine (better than mature red) with cheese.

Any wine sold as 'Nouveau', 'Primeur' or 'Novello' should be in this style. Simple young red Bordeaux should be, too. And if young Midi or Rhône wine is like this you have hit a good one. The lively Cabernet reds of Anjou and Touraine are often of this character – growing redder and more serious only in warm vintages. The best of France's many new 'vins du pays' qualify in the same way. Italy offers Valpolicella, Bardolino and Chiaretto in this style, and sometimes a vivid Dolcetto from Piedmont, too. Lambrusco, traditionally at least, is this kind of wine with bubbles.

Spain or Portugal make fresh young reds only on their Atlantic coast. Few people know that the bulk of Portugal's vinho verde is red; tourists find it a bit rough and ready. Making such fresh and lively red as this is still a challenge that California, Australia and South Africa have to face.

Standard low-price reds, whether sold in jug, bag or bottle

This was once the most popular of all classes of wine, but is now losing ground to whites and the foregoing fresher and fruitier type. Most of these wines are blended to be just sufficiently tasty, reasonably smooth, moderately

Tasting the Beaujolais Nouveau in Beaune. Beaujolais is the classic *vin nouveau*, made to be drunk just after the vintage, but many other French regions now market wines of this increasingly fashionable style.

Burgundy in a silver tastevin, showing traces of sediment. The rich, smooth quality expected of burgundy is seldom a product of nature; more often of judicious blending.

An informal meal at Lorcières in the Auvergne, with a jugful of jug wine. The ideal wine for such an occasion is young, fruity and lively – not heavy, nor too strong.

alcoholic, and a decent shade of red. What they tend to lack is charm, vitality and (inevitable in a blend) any memorable individuality. French versions tend to be dry and rather thin and watery, Italian and Spanish a shade softer and stronger, Californian distinctly sweeter.

Any pretension in serving them (unless as a joke) is quite out of place. To a Frenchman or an Italian they are like the Englishman's cup of tea – always on tap. For refreshment's sake, serve them on the cool side.

It is worth noting that the official EEC category of 'table wine', which covers this no-pretensions department, also covers any wine made outside the framework of national denominations. It is one of the many lunacies of Brussels that, for example, several of Italy's most distinguished wines, made with a wholly justified scorn for the official DOC system, are ranked in EEC language as 'vino da tavola'.

Medium-bodied reds made for maturing

A pretty dull definition of some of the greatest of all red wines: red Bordeaux and burgundy, Rhônes and Riojas, the finest Cabernets and Pinot Noirs of California, the Northwest and Australia, top Chianti Classicos and such specialties as Sassicaia and Tignanello, Torgiano and Carmignano. Portugal enters its best garrafeiras from Dão, Douro and Bairrada, Spain the cream of Penedés reds, Chile, South Africa and New Zealand their fast-improving Cabernets. Their common characteristic is that they need time, in barrel and bottle, to fulfil their potential. To drink a great Bordeaux or burgundy before it is at least five years old is to destroy an embryo. Long vatting plumps them up with tannins, pigments and all manner of tasty stuff. Time moulds these elements into what has been called 'a chemical symphony'. Harmony between the component flavours is

Sampling sherry at the fountainhead in Jerez de la Frontera, Spain. Sherry ranges in style from the crisp, delicate fino to the rich, dark oloroso.

what you are waiting for. The dark deposit you inevitably find in wines of this class is the fall-out from these changes.

Don't overwhelm their flavours with the strongest-tasting dishes. Roast meats are excellent, poultry, too, but not well-hung game or any highly seasoned food. Beware also of cheese. Only the mildest cheeses consort well with fine mature red wines.

The darkest, most full-blooded, turbo-powered reds

Mediterranean regions will ripen red grapes to sticky blackness almost every year. In northern Europe it takes an exceptional summer. The result, in either case, is a darker, more potent wine than the normal Bordeaux or burgundy. California's Napa Valley made its name with this type of wine. Most of its growers are now aiming for something more subtle. Châteauneuf-du-Pape and Hermitage, Barolo, Brunello di Montalcino, Vega Sicilia in central Spain, some of Australia's massively succulent Shiraz reds are classics of the genre.

The rare vintages of Bordeaux that reach this degree of concentration have included 1945, 1961 and 1982. Burgundy has enjoyed even fewer super-vintages.

Black and daunting as these wines may be they can be extraordinary drunk young, tannic and almost sweet at the same time. In youth they can even match powerful cheeses. But old, with their colour ebbing and an autumnal smell coming on, they enter another realm of voluptuous sensations.

Wines with added alcohol

'Fortified' or 'dessert' wines – port, sherry, Madeira and their look-alikes – have only one thing in common: they have been topped up with alcohol (brandy or another spirit) to make them stronger. Port is brandied to keep it sweet, sherry to keep it stable. Fortified wines can improve with age for improbable periods. But don't be misled into thinking this includes time decorating the sideboard in a decanter. Like all other wines they fade with long contact with the air.

VI
WINE WITH MEALS

*M*ating and matching, contrasting and complementing. Why port goes with Stilton and claret with wild strawberries. The challenging and often controversial business of putting wine and food together in the ideal combination.

White with fish, red with meat is not a law, like driving on the left when you land at Dover. You are not going to hit anyone coming the other way. But you have to start somewhere. Clichés can be useful.

I have always been guilty, and I suspect I'm not alone, of choosing wines for people rather than wines for dishes. When I am on my own I drink what I feel like drinking. No, it isn't always champagne. When it's a twosome, I find out (if I don't know already) what sort of wine my friend enjoys and buy a bottle. When it's a larger party, a combination of occasion, mood and domestic economy usually narrows the field enough to make choosing fairly easy.

Occasion? Is it a family meal, a business lunch or an evening celebration? Mood? Do I feel lavish, experimental, or do I want to play it safe? Economy? I feel much happier ordering something I can easily afford (especially in restaurants) than going for a mortgage, so to speak.

My attitude to wine comes with seeing it as a social

drink rather than a condiment for food. Committed
foodies may be scandalized, but I find the times are rare
when my choice of wine is guided – rather than simply
influenced – by the precise flavours of a dish.

THE ART OF MATCHMAKING

An impressionistic approach gets you close enough.
You have learned by experience what flavour to expect
in, say, lamb or liver. With experience you learn
approximately what weight and aroma to expect from,
say, a Beaujolais Nouveau, a five-year-old Pomerol or a
two-year-old Sonoma Chardonnay.

All the art of matching wine with food consists of a
moment's imagination – a mental scanning of the two
repertoires. Think of them, if you like, as two colour
wheels. You can turn them until you find a close match,
or a total contrast, or some pleasing combination in
between.

The catch is that you have to have enough experience
of different wines to colour your own wheel. Few people
ever get this far (and winemakers almost never: in
Burgundy all they know is what food tastes good with
burgundy).

The categories of wine outlined in the last chapter are
a start, at least, at devising a wine-wheel. It would be
foolhardy to be categorical in the same way about food.
Rather than make a long mouth-watering list of every
dish, bland and spicy, that I can think of, let us see what
we mean by contrasting flavours, and what matching
them involves.

Contrast (or complement) is epitomized by the
appalling British habit of dousing fatty food with vin-
egary sauces. French fried potatoes with tomato
ketchup and jellied eels with vinegar that tastes like
battery acid from a brown bottle are a couple of gross
examples. A more delicate one is Chablis with shellfish.
Crab and lobster meat is rich, dense and quite detectably
sweet. The clean, slightly tart, mineral flavour of Chablis
whets the appetite for more.

A quite different sort of contrast between food and

wine is found in the German taste for pairing pungent, well-hung game, venison or wild boar with a sweet and velvety Riesling Auslese.

Sancerre on the Loire is known for two famous products: its aromatic, dry, white wine and its salty, crumbly, powerfully goaty cheese. The two are admirably complementary. Sancerre may be a light wine compared with, say, a red burgundy or a red Rhône, but its acidity and aromas fight back at the cheese in an ideal pairing, where a fleshy red wine would be helplessly pinned to the ropes.

The extreme saltiness of real French Roquefort is already in contrast with its luxurious buttery texture. Add the sweetness of Sauternes to the richness of the

The author and dinner guests at home. The art of choosing which wine to serve with a dish is like turning two colour wheels until you find a close match, a total contrast or something in between.

cream and its bite is diminished to agreeable piquancy. The English follow the same principle in drinking fruity port with their highly savoury Stilton.

Closely paired flavours are commoner in practice than complementary ones. Take a couple of examples much favoured in Bordeaux: fragrant flesh of lamb from the riverside marshes with an almost herbal Médoc, or the fat lampreys of the Dordogne stewed in strong St Emilion and served with the same wine on the table. Here the citizens of Bordeaux are matching food and wine in close harmony. Their apparently eccentric choice of Sauternes with dangerously rich foie gras follows the same logic. Even their habit of pouring old claret over wild wood strawberries, in place of cream, is

The Spanish porón was devised to let you drink wine without smelling it in the days of goatskins.

designed to bring out a hint of strawberry in the wine, and no doubt vice versa – you have to taste this combination to believe it.

PROBLEM PAIRINGS

There is a handful of flavours that never seem to work with wine. Oily smoked fish, such as smoked salmon, is difficult, but try fino sherry with it. Asparagus is also not easy: fat Chardonnays work best. Chocolate is the most notorious: neither pairing nor contrasting ever made a wine even recognizable with dark chocolate creams. Citrus fruit is very tricky. You can drink sweet wines with, say, caramelized oranges, but the wine almost disappears. Sweet dishes in general tend to come off better than any sweet wines chosen to partner them. To taste port or Madeira or old Sauternes at their best try the contrast of a plain sponge cake, or a plate of filberts.

In the same way there are whole cultures of cookery that are, at least on the face of it, inimical to wine. Oriental food, whether Indian, Chinese, Japanese or any other, relies on flavourings that smother the taste of wine. Nobody knows for sure whether the almost total absence of wine in the cultures of the East is due to the native seasonings or the physique of the inhabitants or both. But any choice of wine with fully seasoned oriental food should take into account that the wine will come off second best, if you can taste it at all.

And just as food can smother the flavour of wine, so can another wine which is more full-bodied or flavoury. Tradition has handed down to us a commonsensical order of play in which light wines come before weightier ones. This is often interpreted to mean that all (dry) whites should precede all reds. As the categories above show, however, there are light reds and weighty whites. Let the volume of flavour, not the colour, be the guide.

Convention also decrees that in a meal with two similar wines – say two red Bordeaux of about the same quality but different ages – the younger should be served before the older. This is despite the fact that the older may be more faded and, in practice, lighter. There is good sense in the tradition: the more complex flavours of the older wine would make the younger taste simplistic and two-dimensional if it were served after. In practice I often prefer to serve the two similar wines side by side, or in quite rapid succession, so that friends can enjoy comparing and contrasting.

A bottle of St-Pourçain, a light red from the Upper Loire, strikes the right note with bread and cheese.

VII
TACTICS IN THE RESTAURANT

*H*ouse wines and other gambits. Coping with a wine list, ordering and testing a bottle, contending with overbearing wine waiters and generally holding your own when lunching or dining out.

Whatever feelings of indecision you may have about wine at home, they suddenly come to a head when you go to a restaurant. An unfamiliar wine list and thirsty guests puts you on the spot. Traumatic confrontations with wine waiters are almost part of folklore. But the popular image of a wine waiter as an omniscient being breathing fire and brimstone is very far from the truth. He probably knows considerably less about wine than you do. It is the way he stands at your elbow, a study in controlled impatience, that makes the wine list seem endless.

Where is the best place to start? By asking for a copy of the wine list with, or preferably before, the menu so that you have time to size it up and settle on a strategy.

The conventional round of 'cocktails' gives you a few minutes to get the measure of the list and some idea of the restaurant's skill and interest in wine.

A very long wine list does not necessarily mean that every wine is carefully chosen – or stored. It may have no 'depth' at all — just one bottle each of innumerable famous wines which are replaced individually as (or indeed if) they are sold. With a few celebrated exceptions, where wine is the proprietor's genuine passion, very long lists should be regarded with suspicion. More impressive and reliable is the relatively short list which makes it clear that the person in charge has tasted and chosen all the wines and is prepared to take responsibility for them. A good wine list is fully specific about the origin of each wine: its vintage (never '1976/ 77' as though the year did not matter) and its producer. The name 'Chablis' alone means nothing. 'Chablis' with the name of a grower (whether you have heard of him or not) and a recent vintage is an indication that the list is compiled with care and revised regularly. If the list is vague, don't hesitate to ask to see the label of a bottle which might interest you – and reject it if it is not what you had hoped.

OPENING GAMBITS

A simple but effective dodge for establishing a bridge-head, for getting an instant reference point on the capabilities of a restaurant's wine buyer, is to order a glass of the house white wine. A poor, flat or sharp house wine is a warning not to pin too much faith on the rest of the wine list. A delicious brisk and fruity one is an incitement to investigate what other good things are on offer – or alternatively to order more of the same.

There is a temptation to make an impression on entering a strange restaurant by ordering champagne. Apart from the uplift of drinking it, the way it is served is another useful way of gauging the competence of the cellarer. A good restaurant has champagne (not necessarily of every brand) already cooled. A long wait followed by a great palaver with ice buckets indicates that it is rarely asked for – and may well be stored too long, and too warm. If (and it still happens surprisingly often) the waiter brings shallow 'coupes' instead of deep-bowled 'flutes' or 'tulips' don't hesitate to ask for the restaurant's regular wineglasses instead.

It's just possible that the wine waiter will be an expert. But, sadly, he is quite likely to know less than you do. And it's odds-on that the person who drew up the wine list knew about as much as the wine waiter. A list displays not just wine but also signs that tell you whether or not to put your trust in it. Here is a list of very uneven reliability, showing the kind of points to watch out for.

Lack of detail is the key wine-list sin. This means nothing. Whose Chablis? From which vintage?

Sancerre is from the Loire. Yet that doesn't stop some restaurants from moving it to Burgundy.

This is the way to do it! Wine, status, vintage, producer – all clear to see.

Suspect these wide, anonymous district names. There are plenty of more individual wines about.

Is this German at all? Such made-up names often camouflage Euro-blends.

Better value — at least Liebfraumilch has, by German law, to be Quality wine.

Too general to be much help. Again, whose wine, which vintage?

W·I·N·

WHITE WINES

France: Burgundy

Chablis

Sancerre

Chablis Premier Cru
Monts de Milieu,
1981, Albert Pic

Bourgogne Blanc
Meursault 1981

Bordeaux

Entre-Deux-Mers
Graves AC

Germany

Zellarblumchen

Liebfraumilch

Moselle

Wiltinger Scharzberg,
1981/83

Nowhere near Bordeaux, of course. Yet this mistake occurred at a very expensive restaurant.

Suspicious minds might decide this wine is here to deceive the ignorant who have vaguely heard of a château called Margaux. Ordinary AC Margaux will probably be rather expensive for its quality.

L · I · S · T

RED WINES

France: Bordeaux

Côtes de Provence AC
Médoc
Margaux
Château Bel-Air
Château Haut-Sarpe
   1975/77

France: Burgundy

Beaujolais
Macon
Nuits St Georges
Pommard
Beaune Clos du Roi
   1978, Pierre Ponelle

A château – but which one? There are 30 'Bel-Airs' in Bordeaux. Without an appellation to guide us this could be any of them, from the famous to the obscure.

The vintage trap again: 75 and 77 St-Emilions are respectively superb and indifferent. Which are you paying for?

These easy-to-pronounce names sell a lot of mediocre Burgundy. Here it's crucial to know whose name is on the label.

Beware of the hedged vintage – 81 and 83 from the Saar would be quite different tastes.

Village, vintage, vineyard and merchant: all we need to order with confidence.

Champagne (as Sam Weller noted) can give you 'werry gentlemanly ideas'. It also tends to give a restaurateur certain expectations of you. To revert to a carafe of the house wine afterwards is not only a gastronomic anticlimax; it takes a modicum of moral courage too. My rule is to behave in a restaurant as I do in an auction room: have a clear idea of what I can reasonably afford to spend, given the company and the class of restaurant, and then use the righthand column to limit my choice to a comfortable level. I probably survey the heights of the list, too. It is always a pleasure even to read the name of Château Lafite. But unless the company, the occasion and the restaurant are quite exceptional I would never dream of ordering the grandest wines in a restaurant, where they are marked up to at least twice, sometimes four or five times, their real value. The best place to drink the finest and rarest wines is undoubtedly in your own home.

ONE WINE OR TWO?

On most occasions the choice of food will take precedence over the choice of wine. But this doesn't mean that wine need be an afterthought. The menu and

The first course, in this case a paté, is a good opportunity to test the calibre of the restaurant's cellar by ordering a glass of the house white wine.

the wine list are natural partners. There is time over a leisurely meal to enjoy at least two food-and-wine partnerships. The convention of drinking white wine first, and following it with red, is not only good sense for the wines but fits a wide range of menus.

What to do if one person in a party of, say, four or six has chosen a dish that really calls for white wine, while the rest would prefer red with the *daube de boeuf*? If the party has started with a bottle of white there may well be enough left for an extra glass or two for the fish-eater. If it has all gone, there is the alternative of ordering a glass or a small carafe of the house white, or a half-bottle of something more individual. Unfortunately most wine lists are lamentably short of half-bottles. Restaurants are the very place where they can be most useful.

A couple dining together, and taking all evening over it, will usually find it no struggle to drink a whole bottle of wine. If a drink before dinner is included, it is quite realistic to think of two. If you have chosen different menus, there is no law that says you must compromise and drink the same wine. One of you can carry on with the white wine you had as an appetizer, the other can start a bottle of red – which you both finish with the cheese. It is always a mistake, though, to have wine as the only drink on the table: you will find yourself quenching your thirst with it, rather than enjoying it for its scents and flavours. Order a bottle or jug of water to drink alongside your wine. It will reduce your wine consumption by keeping your thirst at bay.

TESTING THE WINE

You order a bottle. The waiter brings it to your table. He should show you the label, not just in courtesy, but to give you a chance to see that it tallies with the list. If there is a difference, in vintage date or producer, you have the option of accepting it or ordering another wine – which means another rummage through the wine list. For this reason I usually make a mental note of another wine on the list that I would settle for if my first choice turned out to be a dud.

A couple dining together need not stick to the same wine. One can drink white with the main course. The other can start a bottle of red, which both finish with the cheese.

For obvious reasons the cork and capsule should be in place when you first see the wine and the waiter should remove them in your sight. He then gives the host an inch or so of wine to taste, and should, in conventional restaurants, offer the cork as well. Ignore the cork and taste the wine. If it smells sweet and clean, all is well. If it smells mouldy, you have the one-in-a-hundred bad luck of a 'corky' or 'corked' bottle. Sniff the cork: it will smell mouldy, too. It's the mouldy cork that has infected the wine. Nothing can be done except open another bottle, which a decent restaurant will do without demur.

But there are other ways in which individual bottles can occasionally go wrong. If a young white wine is yellowish or brownish and tastes flat (or if champagne has no bubbles) you've got a perfectly good reason for rejecting it. If the wine is an old one it is at your own risk. If on the other hand the taste is simply not what you were expecting, the lesson is at your expense – unless you are on very good terms with the management, or you are ready for a very long discussion.

The question of temperature is entirely at your discretion. Many restaurants bring an ice bucket to keep white wine cool as a matter of course. The first sip will tell you whether it is cold enough for your liking. If it is (and some restaurants serve white wines too icy to taste properly) you can ask the waiter to leave the bottle on the table. (In hot weather it is wise to leave it in the bucket.) Pour from it when you like, notwithstanding the fuss that some waiters make in rushing up to pour for you. It is your wine, and you can do what you like with it.

TO DECANT OR NOT TO DECANT

Most restaurants seem to have a fixed policy about decanting red wine. With many it is yes with Bordeaux, no with burgundy. Burgundy they prefer to serve in a decanting cradle; a certain recipe for muddy wine, with all the sediment stirred in each time the bottle is tipped. Be firm. Never let a waiter pour into glasses from a cradle. If the wine needs a cradle it needs decanting. Otherwise it should be stood upright.

If you choose a wine which you would decant at home, either because it has sediment, or you believe it would improve with aeration, ask the wine waiter to decant it for you. If he raises an eyebrow, or looks surly or sheepish, it may be because he is pressed for time, or possibly because he is not proud of his decanting skills.

In these circumstances you may quite reasonably say that you are prepared, or would prefer, to decant it yourself. Ask for the bottle in a cradle, a carafe and a candle. Let the waiter open the bottle for you in the usual way, while you discreetly sniff the carafe to make sure it is clean and fresh. Then take the bottle and decant it, being careful to leave the dregs. Remember the watchword: you are buying the wine; you can do what you like with it. Keep it under your control. Respect a wine waiter who clearly knows his job – but be wary. He is one of a rare breed.

VIII
SPECIAL OCCASIONS

*P*arties and picnics, barbecues and beanfeasts, functions and fireside tête-à-têtes . . . how to choose the right wine for the right occasion, and how to make sure that you don't run out.

There is no such thing as the 'correct' wine for a particular occasion, just as there are no hard and fast rules for matching wine with food. To put it another way, there is an occasion for every wine, but many possible wines for any occasion. In choosing which wine the occasion demands one has to rely on general guidelines based on tradition, experience, individual preference – and common sense.

WINE BEFORE MEALS

A clever fellow coined the phrase 'the thinking man's martini'. A glass of white wine, the implication goes, is not a 'drink' in the drinking man's sense. But it is. I don't know how deep your martinis are, but five ounces – a decent glass – of French or California (not German) white wine are exactly as strong as one and a half of gin – the normal barman's measure. In terms of pure alcohol, a drink is a drink, whether it be wine, whisky or indeed beer. The differences between drinks and their effects have more to do with factors such as timing (how quickly you swallow a given dose) and, more important still, alcoholic content. Most important of all is whether a drink is combined with food.

Wine is the 'drink of moderation'. Why? Not because it is weaker, but because it belongs with food. To introduce a note of sombre realism, road casualty figures paint the picture very clearly. Drink-related accidents are rarely caused by people who have wined and dined. Wined without dining, yes, but more often beered or whiskied without dining.

It is the food that makes the difference. This is partly, perhaps mainly, because it 'lines the stomach' and slows the ingestion of alcohol into the bloodstream. But I suspect that equally important is the fact that when we drink wine and eat at the same time, or sip and nibble, we take in alcohol at a much more leisurely pace. If you quench thirst without satisfying hunger, more drink becomes a substitute for the food you need. You actually quell hunger pangs by drinking more – an almost certain way of taking more alcohol more quickly than you intend.

Wine can be the perfect appetizer. For me champagne beats all other aperitifs by several lengths. But it is no more a 'safe' drink than any other if you swallow glass after glass without accompanying food. Canapés, bread, nuts or crisps are the minimum. Better still, avoid the overlong aperitif session (often caused by late-arriving guests) and sit down promptly to drink your wine (and some water, too) as an appetizing and satisfying part of a leisurely meal.

Which are the best aperitif wines? Anything with a distinct flavour, but not overemphatic, fruity, heavy, oaky or astringent. To me freshness and lightness are prime qualities in an aperitif, so long as there is a definite enough flavour. Good-quality German wines are often perfect to drink before a meal: strong on aroma and with a nice acidic 'cut' that whets the appetite, but relatively low in alcohol. Poor-quality German 'Tafelwein', in contrast, lacks every aperitif quality. It is watery, insipid, vaguely sweet . . . no, thank you.

What makes champagne (or another sparkling wine) so ideal? The answer is its powerful flavour, the result of prolonged fermentation, combined with the 'lift', the zing that the bubbles give it. Champagne has about the same alcohol content as other French white wines, but its alcohol becomes effective more quickly because the dissolved carbon dioxide in the wine goes straight into your bloodstream. Your circulation reacts by speeding up, just as it does when you are running, to exchange carbon dioxide for oxygen. So a faster bloodstream carries the alcohol around your system. You giggle sooner, but the effects pass off more rapidly.

Freshness and lightness, I'll admit, are not everyone's cup of tea. Some people find natural wines insipid on their own. They want more of the feel of alcohol, the warmth that their dosing with spirits give to sherry, port or vermouth. The French reveal an unexpectedly sweet tooth by enjoying port as an aperitif. The Italians evince their craving for bitterness by their wormwood concoctions, their Camparis and Carpanos.

A smooth piece of wineupmanship: a picnic spot where the ground has been prepared in advance – literally – with a strategically buried champagne bottle.

In Spain, and in the Anglo-Saxon countries too, fino sherry is generally agreed to be the finest of aperitifs. Its delicately dry, distinctly savoury, sometimes almost salty flavour does not so much suggest as demand the savoury miniature dishes, the *tapas*, that every Spanish bar so wisely and profitably provides.

WINE AFTER MEALS

Convention shapes our taste. The Japanese day begins with pickled fish, soup and a bowl of rice. The Western dinner ends with sweet wines. We can rationalize it by saying that sugar sates appetite, so (being affluent) we keep it until the last. But the Japanese say the same about rice.

Convention, then, gives us a list of possible end-of-dinner wines. It starts with port, reminds us of Madeira, curtsies to history by including Marsala and Malaga, then passes to Sauternes and all the gold-to-amber products of 'nobly rotten' grapes: Auslese from Germany, Ausbruchs from Austria, late-harvest wines from

Opera-goers picnicking on the grass at Glyndebourne. A light white wine, such as a Sancerre, goes down well in between courses of Mozart or Verdi.

Acharity dinner-dance at Grosvenor House, London. When ordering wine for a big occasion (even if not as lavish as this one) it is wise to assume that each guest will consume about one bottle.

California, Alsace, Australia, moelleux from the Loire valley, decadent butterscotch Tokay.

Under a separate rubric it lists all the world's aromatic muscat wines, from fruity and sparkling Asti Spumante to chocolate velvet from Australia, with a special halo of fashion for France's excellent (and economical) entry, Muscat de Beaumes de Venise. They are all good in their way. There is only one conventionally accepted dessert wine which I, personally, find unsatisfactory, and that is sweet champagne. Even bottles labelled 'Rich' are never sweet enough for their intended use. I take issue with French taste here as I do over aperitifs. Champagne and desserts should be kept apart.

Are these sweet wines meant to partner food, or to drink on their own? They work well either way. It is not always easy to match two sweet tastes successfully: one must be allowed to dominate. If the dessert does, the wine might as well be sugared water. A good dish for a sweet wine should be a simple, and not a very sugary, one. The stress should be on richness rather than

sweetness. A plain apple tart with buttery pastry gives any sweet wine a perfect background: a lemon meringue pie can only fight the wine, and probably win.

In such cases the logical procedure is to eat the dessert first, drink a glass of water, and then enjoy sipping the wine.

Separated from a direct match with sweet food, the list of possible choices goes far beyond the conventional. Any wine you drink after eating needs to be good. It needs more substance or flavour than it could get away with before the meal. This said, almost anything goes. A mature bottle of red wine or a fine delicate Riesling can be equally satisfying.

And after the meal is a good time to celebrate with a bottle of champagne.

WHEN A LITTLE GOES A LONG WAY

The First Law of Oenoconomy runs like this: the better a wine is, the less of it you need. It sounds a bit strange: surely you will want more? But no, it is poor wine that is unsatisfying, making you go on drinking in the hope of finding the flavour that isn't there. Really good wine satisfies with each sip. In terms of flavour per unit of volume, great wine beats ordinary wine by a factor of, I would say, about ten to one – both in the strength of the flavour and, even more importantly, in its length in your mouth.

This means each sip need only be one-tenth the size to make the same impression. Allow for the fact that the impression is delicious, and you want, shall we say, four times as much of it, you still only need four-tenths as much volume. Translated into bottles, this means that one bottle of truly fine wine will go as far as two and half of plonk – no wonder they sell it in gallon jugs.

The French have a measure for the all-important factor of length of flavour – the time the taste persists after you have swallowed the wine. They call it a 'caudalie'. One caudalie (from the Latin cauda, meaning a tail) equals one full second of lingering flavour. If you take a stopwatch to, say, a plain Bordeaux rouge and a

Lunch break for a boat party on a tour of the port vineyards along the Douro river in Portugal. The fare includes red wine and sardines – not the most conventional match, but the true taste of the country.

(mature) First Growth you will see that the Bordeaux rouge clocks up between one and two seconds before its taste disappears, while the Mouton-Rothschild perfumes your breath for ten, twelve, even twenty or more seconds. It is not only scarcity value, but mathematical logic that sets the price of Mouton ten times or more above its humble rival.

How, then, do you calculate how much wine you are going to need for a given occasion? A rough rule of thumb, used in manuals for caterers, is that you need an average of one and a half glasses of an aperitif per person, followed by two glasses of wine with a meal, and possibly one more after the meal. A 75 centilitre (24 ounce) wine bottle gives six 4-ounce portions. If the aperitif, the table wine and after-dinner wine are all of 'normal' strength the total consumption is, therefore, four and a half glasses or three-quarters of a bottle.

If you serve two or three different wines with the meal, the probability is that guests will drink an extra glass, bringing their total consumption up to nearly a

Red wine and hunting pink at the opening meet of the Heythrop Hunt in the Cotswold hills.

These brave picnickers in the rain at least don't have to worry about keeping their wine cool. On a sunnier

bottle a head. Spread over the whole length of an evening this is not an excessive amount.

Whatever caterers' manuals say, however, there is another phenomenon to be observed: the more people there are in a party the more each person is likely to drink. When you are on your own half a bottle seems enough wine, but when there are two of you one bottle scarcely seems enough. Likewise two bottles can seem meagre for three people – they often feel like a third. Certainly four people need three, and can run to four. I have always supposed that the difference is accounted for by the energy you expend in conversation – that, and

...ay the solution would be an
...nsulated wine cooler or,

better still, a chattering stream
nearby.

...he time you spend over the meal.

Catering for a bigger party I usually assume that
...uests will somehow consume approximately one bottle
...f wine per head in total. This doesn't mean that I open
...hat many bottles. I just make sure they're there.

And if wine is the main event, not supporting a meal
...ut starring at a party with only canapés, or cheese, what
...hen? For a start, choose a wine of moderate flavour and
...trength. Germany makes ideal wines for the solo spot,
...t every degree of sweetness, nearly always moderate in
...lcohol but in good examples wonderfully definite and
...lean-cut in flavour. They manage to keep your interest

and to go on being refreshing, without becoming too much of a good thing. But I must stress that I am talking about German quality wines, at least QbA level and preferably QmP, Kabinett wines – not watery, sugary Tafelwein. The recently introduced Landwein can be more than adequate, too.

Wines in the German style that achieve the same general effect, usually with two or three degrees more alcohol, come from Austria, north-east Italy (especially the Italian Tirol or Alto Adige), northern Yugoslavia, parts of Hungary, and very notably from Australia. Barossa Valley Riesling from South Australia can be a great success at this sort of stand-up party. Among French wines I would choose the aromatic sort: Alsace's Edelzwicker or dry Muscat or a Sauvignon Blanc from Touraine or Bordeaux or Poitou. I would tend away from Chablis or Muscadet or Mâcon Blanc which can become a bit tiring to drink without food. Italy has dozens of very pleasant dryish white wines that score well at parties: notably Pinot Grigios from the north-east, Soave Classico, Frascati and such modern Tuscan whites as Galestro. Spain's Penedés whites are also on about the right scale. The very light, slightly fizzy vinho verde of Portugal creates a certain exotic atmosphere but

Watching international rowing from the Stewards' Enclosure at Henley Royal Regatta (*left*). Summer outdoor events of this kind demand a festive, refreshing drink such as champagne or an iced wine cup.

An inflatable dinghy filled with ice (*right*) makes a practical champagne cooler at one of the yacht club balls during the annual Cowes Week yachting regatta on the Isle of Wight.

becomes faintly unsatisfying after two or three glasses.

Of California wines, several makes of 'Chablis' are sound, if not very exciting or original. A good Chenin Blanc or French Colombard could be an improvement, or a Riesling better still. Chardonnay (and even Fumé Blanc) tend to be overweighty for party drinking – at least to my taste. California wines are not on the whole as thirst-quenching as wines from Europe: an essential quality in a good party wine.

There are fewer reds that have the easy-going, refreshing, moderate degree of flavour that make them drink well over a period of time without food. The sort of tannin that makes deep-coloured young reds astringent turns your tongue and gums to leather after a bit. Beaujolais, rapidly fermented and only slightly tannic, flows well. Beaujolais-Villages flows better. Light young Côtes-du-Rhône reds are tolerable, but the sort of cherry-reds such as Valpolicella, Bardolino and Chiaretto of north-east Italy can be better. I stress the 'can'. There is a lot of rubbish sold under the name of Valpolicella. In California I would choose a light Zinfandel – not always easy to find – or a well-made red blend, whether marketed under the name of 'Burgundy' or 'Mountain Red'.

Making mulled wine, an ideal concoction for winter drinking. My recipe is to start with red wine, adding orange and lemon juice, sugar, cloves, cinammon and some spirits – preferably an orange liqueur.

The most valuable role of red wine at parties is in cold weather, when it becomes the basis for what the British call mulled wine, the Germans *Glühwein*. The principle is simple: red wine mixed with orange and lemon juice (and zest), sweetened with sugar syrup, strengthened with brandy and spiced with cloves and cinnamon. It is a happy winter ritual, slowly simmering the wine in a huge pan, tasting as you go, adjusting the ingredients. Experience has taught me never to let the mixture boil, and to use an orange liqueur such as Grand Marnier in preference to brandy – added at the last minute.

The summer version of the same drink is Sangria: red wine and oranges, iced. So much watery and acidic liquid has been baptised with the name that I hesitate to mention how good it can be, freshly made with full-bodied red wine, sweet oranges, a little sugar and ice added only in large lumps.

The wine that is purpose-built for parties, though, is champagne, or any of the countless sparkling wines made in almost every region today by the champagne method. The frivolity of fizz is its essential quality. It does not need to be the most expensive brand for a party – any party, even if you can afford it. Great bottles of vintage champagne deserve more reverential treatment at a more intimate occasion.

Despite the immense improvement in quality of sparkling wines other than champagne, people still sometimes hide the label of, say, a sparkling Loire or white burgundy, as though they were cheating their guests. Californians know better and serve their native sparklers with pride.

For an afternoon party (which many weddings are) very dry champagne is out of place. Demi-sec champagnes are not usually as good, in my experience, as some of the attractively fruity Crémants (top-quality sparklers) of Alsace, the Loire or Burgundy, or a good German Sekt. Italian and Spanish sparkling wines (the Spanish call the good ones, generically, 'cava') tend to be made extremely dry – I am not thinking of Asti-Spumante, the best really sweet fizz of all. The ready way of making a delicious and less potent party drink was invented at the turn of the century by, I believe, the barman at Buck's Club in London. 'Buck's Fizz' is champagne with fresh-squeezed orange juice.

Someone more recently transferred to sparkling wine the essentially tranquil idea of a great Burgundian priest and war hero, the Canon Kir, who liked his dry, acidic white Aligoté enriched with a drop or two of crème de cassis, the blackcurrant cordial of his home town, Dijon. A 'Kir Royale' is champagne and cassis. Come to that, a 'King's Peg', regal reviver of jaded professors at Cambridge (King's College claims the invention) is the same idea with vintage champagne and a lovely old pale vintage cognac as its ingredients.

What times!

GLOSSARY

· A ·

Acetic

Unless wine is protected from the oxygen in the air its bacteria will rapidly produce volatile acetic acid, giving it a faint taste and smell of vinegar.

Acidity

Don't knock it. At least half a dozen different acids are essential for zest, freshness, liveliness, aroma, longevity – the best wines have plenty of acid balanced by plenty of stuffing. You taste too much acid in poor wines because the stuffing is missing.

Aftertaste

The flavour that lingers in your mouth after a sip. Scarcely noticeable (and occasionally unpleasing) in a poor wine; deliciously haunting in a great one. (See *caudalie*.)

Age

Not necessarily a good thing. Cheap wines in general want drinking young. See *pages 26–28*.

Alcohol

Between 7% and 25% of a wine is alcohol, with most tables wines in the range $10\frac{1}{2} – 13\frac{1}{2}\%$. During fermentation all or some of the sugar in the grapes is converted into ethyl alcohol, which acts as a preservative and gives the wine its 'vinosity', or winey-ness.

Amontillado

A matured fino sherry, naturally dry but generally sweetened to be mellow in taste.

Appellation d'origine contrôlée (AOC)

Official rank of all the best French wines, meaning 'controlled designation of origin', usually shortened to 'Appellation contrôlée' (AC). On a label, this guarantees both place of origin and a certain standard.

Aroma

The primary smell of a young wine, compounded of grape juice, fermentation and (sometimes) the oak of a barrel.

Astringent

Dry quality, causing the mouth to pucker – the result of high tannin or acid content.

Auslese

German for 'selection'. Refers to a category of QmP (qv) white wine made of grapes selected for ripeness above a statutory level, depending on the region. A good Auslese benefits from ageing for several years in bottle.

· B ·

Balance

The all-important ratio between the different characteristics of a wine, such as fruitiness, sweetness, acidity, tannin content and alcoholic strength. These should harmonize like the various sounds in a symphony.

Balling

An American measure of ripeness in grapes, and hence potential alcohol in wine. Also known as Brix.

Balthazar

A monster champagne bottle, equivalent to 16 ordinary bottles.

Barrel

Not an anachronistic container but a vital part of the stabilizing and early ageing process for most of the world's best wines.

Barrique

The standard Bordeaux barrel, holding 225 litres.

Basket

See cradle.

Beerenauslese

German for 'grape selection'. A category of QmP (qv) wine, sweeter and more expensive than Auslese because only the ripest bunches are used. Ages admirably.

Beeswing

A kind of deposit sometimes found in port, so called because of the veined pattern which it forms.

Bereich

A large area, although smaller than a 'region', in Germany. Bernkastel and Johannisberg are Bereich (as well as village) names, greatly increasing the amount of these fashionable wines available.

Bin

A section of a cellar devoted to one wine – hence 'bin-ends' for oddments on sale.

Bitterness

A taste not usually found in good wines – although some young tannins can be bitter – but a characteristic aftertaste of many north-east Italian wines such as Valpolicella.

Blackcurrants
A smell and flavour characteristic of wines made from Cabernet Sauvignon and sometimes Sauvignon Blanc grapes.

Blend
Nearly every wine involves some blending, whether it be of grapes, vintages or the contents of different vats. With fortified wines blending is almost universal. But blends of wines from different regions or countries tend to lack character.

Bodega
Spanish word meaning a large storage vault, a wine-producing establishment or a bar.

Botrytis cinerea
The so-called 'noble rot', a mould which has the effect of concentrating the sugar and flavouring substances in grapes by allowing the evaporation of the water in the juice. Under controlled conditions it is used to produce sweet white wines of the highest quality (e.g. in Sauternes).

Botrytized
Affected by the botrytis mould. A regrettable American neologism.

Bottle-age
The length of time a wine has been kept in bottle (rather than in the cask).

Bottle-sickness
A (usually) temporary setback in a wine's flavour for weeks or months after bottling.

Bottle-stink
A bad smell sometimes found on opening old bottles, which almost instantly dissipates. It can be confused with 'corkiness' – but only for a few minutes.

Bouquet
The characteristic smell of a matured wine, by analogy with a posy of flowers. Strictly speaking not the same as aroma (qv).

Breathing
What wine does if you expose it to the air by decanting it a few hours before drinking. Opinions are divided as to whether wine benefits from breathing. See pages 45 and 48–49.

Breed
A certain kind of polish and distinction in a wine. Found only in impeccably made wines from very good vineyards. A rather difficult word to use without feeling foolish.

Brix
See balling.

Brut
Extremely dry. Usually used only in connection with champagne.

Butt
A sherry or whisky cask holding 491 litres.

· C ·

Carafe
Stopperless container used for serving wine at table. The 'carafe wine' in a restaurant is the standard house wine.

Cask
Wooden barrel used for storing wine or spirit. Casks come in many sizes and have different names depending on what they contain. A sherry cask is a 'butt'; a port cask is a 'pipe'.

Caudalie
French measure of the length of time the aftertaste of a wine lasts.

Cave
French for cellar.

Chai
Storage building of a château or wine estate (especially in Bordeaux) where wine is kept in cask.

Chambrer
To bring wine to room temperature. See page 55.

Chaptalization
The addition of a small permitted amount of sugar during fermentation in order to boost the alcoholic strength of a wine.

Character
Term of praise indicating that a wine has a distinctive and individual stamp.

Château
Used in a wine context, this means either the country house or mansion of a wine-producing estate or the estate as a whole. On a French label it means that the wine comes solely from that estate.

Château-bottled
Bottled on the estate rather than by the merchant. Other things being equal, château-bottled wines are generally valued higher, whether or not their quality justifies it.

Chill
See pages 54–55.

Claret
English term for the red wines of Bordeaux.

Classé
'Classed'. There have been many classifications of the vineyards of France, the most famous that of certain Bordeaux châteaux in 1855. Each important area of France has its own 'classed growths', or their equivalents, but there is no unifying system. The term is most often used about Bordeaux.

Clavelin
Dumpy, old-fashioned bottle used in France's Jura.

Climat
Burgundian word for an individual vineyard site.

Colour
See pages 62–66.

Commune
The French for parish. Many wines bear the name of a parish rather than an individual grower (e.g. St-Julien, St-Emilion, Pommard).

Cooperage
General term for wooden containers. A cooper is a barrel-maker (and a rich man these days).

Cork
See *pages 9–11*.

Corkage
Charge made by a restaurant to those who bring their own wine.

Corky or corked
Contaminated by a rotten cork, resulting in an unpleasant taste.

Coulant
'Flowing'. French term for easy-to-drink wines, such as Beaujolais.

Coulure
A condition of the vine at flowering time, causing the grapes to fall off prematurely.

Courtier
French term for a wine broker.

Cradle
A device for holding a bottle in a near-horizontal position so that it can be opened and poured without the deposit being disturbed, usually for decanting purposes. The basket fulfils a similar function.

Crémant
Indicating a degree of sparkle, less than mousseux but more than perlant or pétillant.

Cru
French word for 'growth', applied to the produce of a vineyard or group of vineyards making wine of a particular character.

Crust
A type of heavy deposit found particularly in bottles of vintage port.

Cuvée
The contents of a cuve *(vat). It can also mean a quantity of blended wine.*

· D ·

Decant
To transfer wine from a bottle to a stoppered flask (decanter). See pages 44–49.

Demi
Half.

Demijohn
A type of large bottle, usually encased in wickerwork and holding at least a gallon (4.5 litres). The name probably derives from the French Dame Jeanne.

Demi-sec
French for 'half dry'. The term is usually applied to sparkling wines and means that sugar has been added to produce a degree of sweetness, sometimes marked.

Deposit
High-quality wines maturing in bottle almost always develop a greater or lesser deposit, the fall-out from chemical changes which give them greater character, complexity and bouquet.

Disgorge
Refers to the champagne method of making sparkling wines. At one point the bottle has to be opened to remove a deposit of yeasty sediment. French 'dégorgement'.

DOC
Official Italian wine classification,

similar in some ways to the French AOC. It stands for Denominazione di Origine Controllata (controlled denomination of origin). In practice it means very little.

DOCG
The top category of Italian wines, theoretically superior to DOC as indicated by the addition of the letter G for garantita (guaranteed).

Domaine
A (wine-producing) property. This is the normal word in Burgundy, whereas in Bordeaux they use the term 'château'.

Dosage
The sweetening added to sparkling wine before the final corking.

Double magnum
A four-bottle bottle, three litres of wine.

Dry
A relative term, implying the opposite of sweet.

· E ·

Einzellage
German term meaning a single, individual vineyard site, as opposed to a Grosslage, a collection of such sites.

Eiswein
Very sweet German wine made by harvesting frozen grapes during a frost and pressing them while still frozen. The flavours and acidity are intensely concentrated and the wine apparently almost immortal.

Elegant
As of a woman, unmistakable but indefinable.

Eleveur
Someone who buys new wine from the grower and prepares (literally 'educates') it for sale.

Enology
See oenology.

Erzeugerabfüllung
Literally 'producer-bottling'. The German equivalent of 'domaine-bottled'.

Extract
Soluble solids from the grape, which contribute to the weight and fullness of a wine.

· F ·

Fass
German for cask.

Fermentation
The conversion of grape juice into wine through the action of certain yeasts present in the juice, which turn sugar into alcohol. See also malolactic fermentation.

Feuillette
A Chablis barrel.

Fiasco
A Chianti flask.

Fine
A general term of approbation denoting overall quality.

Finesse
Literally 'fine-ness'. The word implies subtlety and distinction.

Fining
Method of clarifying wine by pouring a coagulant (e.g. eggwhites, blood) on top and letting it settle to the bottom.

Finish
The final taste left by a sip of wine on swallowing.

Fino
The finest style of sherry – dry, delicate and usually light in colour.

Fliers
Little specks of sediment.

Flute
A tall, narrow, cone-shaped glass, perhaps the prettiest for sparkling wine.

Fortified
Strengthened by the addition of extra alcohol during production.

Foxy
Tasting of native American or 'fox' grapes.

Frais
French term meaning either fresh or cool.

Frappé
French for very cold or iced.

Frizzante
An Italian term meaning slightly sparkling, as opposed to spumante, fully sparkling.

Fruity
Tasting pleasantly of ripe grapes – but a term so widely used as to have little clear meaning.

Füder
Type of cask used for Mosel wine and holding about 960 litres.

Full or full-bodied
Refers to a wine that is high in alcohol and extract, causing it to feel weighty and substantial in the mouth.

Fumé
Literally 'smoky' – refers to the peculiar tangy aroma of certain young wines made from the Sauvignon Blanc, e.g. Pouilly Fumé.

Fût
General French word for a cask.

· G ·

Garrafeira
Portuguese term for a merchant's selection – frequently his best long-matured wine.

Gazéifié
French for fizzy or carbonated.

Generic
In California, the opposite of 'varietal', e.g wine called 'Burgundy' or 'Chablis'.

Grand cru
Literally 'great growth'. Means different things in different regions of France. In Burgundy it is the top rank. In Bordeaux (particularly St-Emilion) almost everything is a 'Grand Cru'.

Grosslage
In German terminology a group of neighbouring Einzellages (qv) of supposedly similar character.

Gutsverwaltung
German for property or estate.

· H ·

Harmony
A highly desirable quality: a balance of attributes.

Hock
British term for the white wines of the Rhine and surrounding areas. It is believed to derive from Hochheim, a town on the Main.

Hogshead
A cask. The size and contents vary depending on where the word is being used. A hogshead of Bordeaux wine, also known as a barrique, contains 225 litres, whereas one of whisky holds 249.2 litres.

Hybrid
Used in wine circles of a cross between French and American vines, designed for hardiness. Hybrids are much used in the eastern USA.

· I ·

Impériale
Outsize Bordeaux bottle, holding about eight ordinary bottles, occasionally used for very fine wines.

· J ·

Jeroboam
Champagne bottle size, containing four normal bottles.

Jug wine
Otherwise known as 'carafe wine'

or 'vin ordinaire' or 'plonk'. Cheap, workaday wine without pretensions to grandeur.

· K ·

Kabinett
The first category of Qualitätswein mit Prädikat, the highest classification of German wine. Kabinett wines are lighter and less expensive than other QmP wines such as Spätlese and Auslese.

Kellerabfüllung
Bottled at the (German) cellar.

Kosher wine
Wine for Jewish religious occasions, made under the supervision of a rabbi. It is usually very sweet.

· L ·

Lagar
The stone trough in which the grapes are (or were) trodden by barefooted workers to make port and other Portuguese wines.

Lage
German term for a particular vineyard.

Lees
Solid residue that remains in the cask after the wine has been drawn off.

Legs
The rivulets that run down the side of a wineglass after swirling. When the legs are pronounced it indicates a wine rich in body and extract.

Light
Possessing a low degree of alcohol or, more loosely, lacking in body.

Limousin
Region of north-central France whose oak forests produce perfect wood for barrels.

Liquoreux
Used of a wine that is rich, sweet and pretty strong too. Sauternes is the classic example.

Litre
Bottle size used mainly for everyday wines. The standard capacity of a wine bottle is $\frac{3}{4}$ litre.

· M ·

Maderized
This term refers to the brown colour and flat taste of a white wine that has been over-exposed to air during production or maturation.

Magnum
Wine bottle holding $1\frac{1}{2}$ litres, the equivalent of two normal bottles.

Malolactic fermentation
A secondary stage of fermentation in which malic acid is converted into lactic acid and carbon dioxide. As lactic acid is milder, the taste of the wine becomes less acid. Some winemakers encourage it, if necessary, by warming the new wine. Others avoid it to keep a sharper acidity.

Marc
The pulpy mass of grape skins and pips left after the fermented grapes have been pressed. Also the name of the strong-smelling brandy distilled from this.

Marque
French for brand. In Champagne the 'Grandes Marques' are the top dozen or so houses.

Méthode champenoise
The 'champagne method'. Used worldwide today to signify the laborious way of making sparkling wine perfected in Champagne.

Methuselah
Not an unusually long-lived wine but a bumper champagne bottle holding eight normal bottles.

Millésime
French for the vintage year (e.g. 1982).

Mise
French word meaning 'putting', used for bottling. The past participle occurs in such phrases as mis en bouteille au château (château-bottled). But sometimes you will see simply mise du château, meaning the same thing.

Moelleux
French for 'marrow-like'. Used of a wine it means soft and rich, particularly of Loire wines such as Vouvray that vary from dry one year to moelleux the next.

Monopole
A wine whose brand name is the exclusive property of a particular firm or grower.

Mousseux
French for sparkling. Not usually used for first-class wines.

· N ·

Nebuchadnezzar
The largest size of champagne bottle, holding the equivalent of 20 ordinary bottles. Named after the colourful king who destroyed Jerusalem and built the Hanging Gardens of Babylon. He would doubtless have appreciated the tribute.

Négociant
French term loosely translated as 'shipper', but implying a dealer who buys wine from the estates and distributes it either wholesale or retail. See also éleveur.

Nerveux
A term of praise implying fineness combined with firmness and vitality.

Noble rot
See Botrytis cinerea.

Nose
Wine jargon for smell, whether aroma or bouquet (qqv).

Nouveau
As in Beaujolais Nouveau – the wine of the last harvest, during its first winter.

· O ·

Oaky
Refers to a wine that has picked up something of the taste and smell of the oak cask in which it was matured. Many producers go to great trouble to obtain the right nuance of oakiness by choosing oak of a certain type for their barrels. See Limousin.

Oechsle
System used in Germany for measuring the proportion of sugar in the must.

Oeil de Perdrix
'Eye of the partridge', a metaphor used to describe the pink colour of certain rosé wines as well as some pink champagnes and even whites with a pinkish tinge.

Oenoconomy
Counting the change (if any).

Oenology
Knowledge or study of wine (from the Greek oinos, wine).

Oenophile
A lover or connoisseur of wines.

Organoleptic
A highfalutin way of saying 'sensory'. Organoleptic evaluation is the judging of a wine by measuring its effect on the different senses.

Originalabfüllung
The German equivalent of mis en bouteille au château. It means 'original bottling' and signifies that the wine has been bottled on the premises by the grower. Originalabzug means the same.

Oxidized
Possessing a stale, flat taste owing to excessive exposure to air. See also maderized.

· P ·

Palo Cortado
A rare and excellent style of sherry, between fino and oloroso.

Passito, Vino
Italian sweet dessert wine made from grapes that have been dried for a short time after picking.

Pasteurization
Process invented by Louis Pasteur (1822–1895) in which substances are sterilized by heat. It is used for certain run-of-the-mill wines, but is not considered desirable for the finer ones.

Pelure d'oignon
Onion skin. This is how the French describe the pale, orange-brown colour of certain rosé wines and some old reds.

Perlant
Showing a slight degree of sparkle, less than crémant and much less than mousseux.

Perlwein
German name for a wine that is pétillant.

Pétillant
Having a very light, natural sparkle, even less pronounced than with a perlant wine.

Phylloxera
An American vine pest accidentally introduced into Europe in the latter part of the 19th century. It destroyed almost all vineyards, not only in Europe but throughout the world, in a disaster without precedent. Most European vines are now grafted on to American phylloxera-resistant stock.

Pied
French for a single vine.

Pipe
A port cask containing 522.48 litres. The word is also used to refer to a Madeira cask containing 418 litres and a Marsala cask holding 422 litres.

Plastering
Not getting someone drunk, but boosting the acid content of a wine by the addition of calcium sulphate (plaster of Paris). The practice is more common in Mediterranean countries (especially in making sherry) where the natural acid content of the wine tends to be low.

Plonk
Slang for everyday wine, possibly a garbled version of blanc, as in vin blanc.

Porón
Double-spouted Spanish drinking vessel which enables the wine to be drunk without the glass touching the lips. When the glass is raised one spout lets out a stream of wine while the other lets in air.

Port
English name for the fortified wine produced on the banks of the Douro river in northern Portugal and matured in the cellars at Vila Nova de Gaia. It is made in both red and white forms.

Pot
A type of large-bellied wine bottle now largely confined to Beaujolais. The brand known as Piat de Beaujolais comes in this type of bottle.

Pourriture noble
See Botrytis cinerea.

Prädikat
See *QmP*.

Premier Cru
*First of the five categories of
Médoc châteaux established by the
classification set up in 1855.
Châteaux in this category are
Château Lafite-Rothschild,
Château Latour, Château
Margaux, Château Mouton-
Rothschild and Château Haut-
Brion.*

Premium
*California term for wines over a
certain fairly modest price – i.e.
the opposite of 'jugs'.*

Pricked
*A useful, if archaic, term for the
unpleasantly sharp quality caused
by the presence of too much
volatile acidity.*

Primeur
*Term applied to certain wines sold
very young, especially Beaujolais.*

Punt
*The hollow mound poking up
inside the bottom of a wine bottle.
Universal in old hand-blown
bottles but now generally limited
to champagne and port.*

· Q ·

QbA
Abbreviation for the term
Qualitätswein eines
bestimmten Anbaugebietes
*(quality wine from a specific
region), the second highest category
of German wine. QbA wines are
closely delimited in their origins
but are made of grapes that*
*ripened insufficiently to make wine
without added sugar – as distinct
from the next category.*

QmP
Qualitätswein mit Prädikat
*(quality wine with special
attributes), the top category of
German wine, made with fully
ripe grapes only. QmP wines are
further categorized as Kabinett
(light and usually fairly dry),
Spätlese (fuller and usually fairly
sweet), Auslese (rich and usually
sweet, sometimes superbly
honeyed), Beerenauslese and
Trockenbeerenauslese (qqv).*

· R ·

Racking
*Transferring the fermented wine
from one cask to another to
separate it from its lees.*

Ratafia
*Brandy mixed with sweet
unfermented grape juice. A
speciality of Champagne.*

Récolte
*French word for the crop or
vintage.*

Rehoboam
*Another of those biblical names
for big champagne bottles. This
one holds six normal bottles.*

Remuage
*Technique invented by the widow
Clicquot in the early 19th century
for removing the deposit in
champagne without removing the
sparkle. It involves shaking and
turning each bottle and inclining it
at a progressively sharper angle*

until it is almost upside down.
This goes on for six weeks or
more until all the deposit has
settled on the cork. Then the cork
is taken out (see 'disgorge') and
the deposit extracted.

Reserva
Italian term for wine that has
undergone a statutory period of
ageing, in length depending on the
DOC (qv).

Réserve
An uncontrolled term implying
superior quality.

Rhenish
Archaic term for Rhine wine.

Riddling
English term for remuage (qv).

Riserva
Spanish equivalent of Reserva,
with similar statutory limits.

Rosato
Italian for rosé.

Rosé
Pink wine made from black
grapes pressed quickly to allow
only some of the skin colour to
tinge the wine. Rosés vary in
colour from deep pink, almost red,
to pale, almost white.

Rosso
Italian for red.

Rouge
French for red.

Ruby
The name given to young red port,
matured in wood, but not for long.

Rurale, méthode
Probably the original way of
making sparkling wine, antedating
the méthode champenoise. Still
used, with modifications, in south-
west France.

· S ·

Sack
Archaic term for sherry and
similar strong wines.

Salmanazar
The third largest size of
champagne bottle, holding 12
normal bottles.

Schaumwein
German for sparkling wine. No
implication of quality.

Schillerwein
A type of German rosé wine,
made from a mixture of black
and white grapes. The name comes
from the word Schiller meaning
lustre and has nothing to do with
the poet Schiller.

Schoppenwein
The 'open' wine sold in a German
Weinstube or tavern.

Sec
In French this word means dry or
fermented out, but in relation to
champagne it is used in a
somewhat specialized way. A very
dry champagne is described as
'brut'. 'Sec' means containing some
added sweetness. 'Demi-sec' means
decidedly sweet. With other wines
the word sec is an indication of
relative rather than absolute
dryness. The same applies to the
Italian word secco.

Secco
See Sec.

Sediment
Solid matter deposited in a bottle
in the course of the maturing
process. Nearly always a good
sign.

Sekt
The German word for sparkling
wine.

Solera
The name for a system of blending
and maturing sherry, also applied
to the storage building where the
process takes place. The sherry is
arranged in different casks
according to age and character, and
the contents of the casks are
transferred and blended according
to complex permutations that vary
from one firm to another.

Sommelier
French term for a wine waiter.

Sparkling
Containing bubbles of carbon
dioxide gas. This condition can be
brought about in three different
ways: (1) fermentation in the
bottle (champagne method); (2)
fermentation in a closed vat
(Charmat method); (3) pumping
CO2 into the wine (rudely called
the Bicycle Pump method).

Spätlese
German term for a wine made
from late-harvested grapes.

Spritzer
A drink made with white wine
diluted with soda or mineral
water.

Spritzig
German adjective to describe a
wine possessing a light, natural
sparkle.

Spumante
Italian for fully sparkling.

Stuck
Of fermentation: the point where,
owing to an uncontrolled rise in
temperature, the yeasts are
overcome by the heat and the
fermentation stops.

Stück
The traditional 1,200-litre cask of
the Rhine.

Sulphur
The most common disinfectant for
wine. It is dusted on to the vines
to prevent fungus, burnt inside
casks to fumigate them and added
to the must, usually in the form of
sulphur dioxide, to destroy
harmful bacteria. Unless it has
been carelessly used the flavour of
the sulphur will not be transmitted
to the wine.

Süss
German for sweet.

Süssreserve
Unfermented, and therefore
naturally sweet, grape juice. Used
in Germany to blend with dry
wines to balance them.

· T ·

Table wine
In common use, this means any
non-fortified wine. In EEC terms
it means a wine below the rank of
VQPRD (qv).

Tafelwein

Deutscher Tafelwein is the lowest of the three categories of German wine. The presence of the word 'deutscher' indicates that the wine is made entirely in Germany. If it is merely called Tafelwein it may be blended with wines from other countries.

Tannin

A substance found in the skins, stalks and pips of the grapes. It is also absorbed into wine from oak casks and is sometimes added artificially. Tannin acts as a preservative and is therefore an important ingredient if the wine is to be matured over a long period. It imparts a hard, dry quality.

Tappit-hen

Pewter vessel holding 4.1 litres, formerly widely used in Scotland. Alternatively, a port bottle holding three normal bottles.

Tartaric

An acid occurring naturally in grapes and the main constituent of the acidity in wine.

Tastevin

Shallow vessel of silver, glass or ceramic, used in Burgundy for sampling wine. Its shape, with indentations and raised boss in the centre, makes it easier to judge the colour of a wine.

Tasting

See 'Judging wine', pages 60–67.

Tawny

The name given to port that has been aged in wood until it has acquired a tawny colour.

Temperature

See pages 28 and 53–55.

Terroir

A French word meaning soil and site. A wine is said to have un gout de terroir (a taste of the soil) when it has gathered certain nuances of taste and flavour from the land on which it was produced.

Tête de cuvée

A term used mainly in the Burgundy area to refer to the 'cream' of the wine sold under a particular name.

Tinto

Spanish for red.

Tirage

French word usually meaning the transfer of wine from cask to bottle. Literally 'drawing off'.

Tischwein

German for table wine. Not an official term (see Tafelwein) but used to refer to ordinary mealtime wines.

Tonne

French for a large cask or container of unspecified size.

Tonneau

A general French term for a cask, but in Bordeaux refers to a quantity of wine, namely 1,000 litres, or 100 cases of wine.

Trocken

German for dry.

Trockenbeerenauslese (TBA)

A category of German wine. It is

made by picking out individual grapes affected by the noble rot, Botrytis cinerea, *resulting in an exceptionally rich, luscious (and expensive) wine.*

Tun
Archaic term for a barrel.

· U ·

Ullage
The amount that would be needed to top a bottle (or barrel) of wine right up to the cork or bung. 'Ullaged' bottles (with empty necks) can be disappointing.

· V ·

Varietal
A varietal wine is one that is named after the grape variety from which it is made.

Vat
Large vessel or tank for fermenting or blending wine. Nowadays vats may be made of wood, concrete or stainless steel, sometimes with a glass lining.

VDQS (Vin Délimité de Qualité Supérieur)
The second official category of French wines, subject to slightly less rigorous regulations than those applying to Appellation Contrôlée wines. The category was set up in 1949 and has since become firmly established.

Vendange
The French word for vintage.

Vendemmia
Ditto in Italian.

Vignoble
French for vineyard.

Vin de garde
A wine whose potential to mature makes it worth keeping.

Vin de l'année
Literally 'wine of the year', that is to say of the current vintage.

Vin de la région
What you ask for when you want a wine made in the region where you happen to be.

Vin de liqueur
This is the French name for what in Britain would be called 'fortified wine', a term which in France would imply an improper addition of alcohol.

Vin de pays
Not to be confused with vin de la région, *this is the third official category of French wines, established in 1976. There are over* 150 *districts, some large (*vin de pays de zone*), some covering* départements (vin de pays départementale), *some (the most interesting), small districts.*

Vin Doux Naturel (VDN)
A description used for a type of wine made in southern France. These wines are high in natural sugar content and are fortified by the addition of extra alcohol, making them about as strong as an average sherry. Drink them as dessert wines, after meals or on their own, like sherry.

Vin jaune
These are white wines with a

yellowish hue caused by bacterial action during the long fermentation process. They have a strong and distinctive flavour and bouquet and are made solely in the Jura region of France.

Vin nouveau
New wine, made to be drunk just after the vintage. Beaujolais is the most famous, but many other French regions now market a nouveau.

Vin ordinaire
Not an official category of French wine but a loose term for basic wine, bought often by the alcoholic degree per litre and regarded as a grocery commodity, not a subject for connoisseurship.

Viña
Spanish for vineyard.

Vinho generoso
Spanish term for aperitif and dessert wines such as sherry.

Vinho verde
A light, tangy wine made in northern Portugal. The name, meaning 'green wine', refers to its newness, not its colour. It comes in both red and white, but the term is mainly associated with the white wine.

Vintage
The annual harvesting and production of a wine. More particularly, a vintage wine is one that bears the date of the vintage on the label, either because it is meant to be drunk young or because it was made to be matured over a number of years.

Viticulture
The science and art of growing grapes.

VQPRD
Vin de Qualité Produit dans une Région Determinée (quality wine produced in a defined zone). This is an EEC quality category. Italian DOC, French AOC and German QbA wines all qualify. In the eyes of Brussels all else is 'table wine'.

· W ·

Weingut
Term used in Germany and Austria for a wine-producing estate that grows its own grapes.

Weissherbst
A type of white wine made in Baden, Germany, from black grapes

Winzergenossenschaft
The German word for a wine cooperative, a group of growers who have clubbed together to produce wine.

· Y ·

Yeast
Collection of micro-organisms which causes fermentation (qv). Wild yeasts are naturally present on grape skins, but special yeasts are usually used.

Yield
The amount of wine produced by a vineyard, usually expressed in hectolitres (100 litres) per hectare or hl/ha. Higher quantity means lower quality or lighter wine which matures more rapidly.

INDEX

ACKNOWLEDGMENTS

Illustrations by Sue Sharples

Photographs
3, 10, 21, 22–23, 32–33, 34–35, 36–37, 38–39,
48, 50–51, 53, 54–55, 56–57, 58–59, 63, 64, 66 Kim Sayer;
94–95, 112, 118–119 Gered Mankowitz
© 1985 Mitchell Beazley Publishers

31 Elizabeth Whiting & Associates; 40–41 Craig Carlson; 72
Berenguier/Jerrican; 73 Paul Fusco/Magnum; 75 Richard Kalvar/Magnum; 76–
77, 78 Bruno Barbey/Magnum; 79 Monique Jacot/Susan Griggs Agency; 80–81
Bruno Barbey/Magnum; 82 Gilles Peress/Magnum; 83 Richard Kalvar/Magnum;
85 René Burri/Magnum; 86 Berenguier/Jerrican; 86–87 Richard Kalvar/Magnum;
88 Fred Mayer/Magnum; 96 Tor Eigeland/Susan Griggs Agency; 97 Bertrand
Duruel/Explorer; 104, 106 The Anthony Blake Photo Library; 113, 114–115
Julian Calder; 116–117 Anthony Howarth/Susan Griggs Agency; 117 Adam
Woolfitt/Susan Griggs Agency; 120, 121 Patrick Ward/Susan Griggs Agency

Picture Research by Brigitte Arora